JESUS BURGERS

VOLUME TWO

IMPACTING A GENERATION ONE LIFE AT A TIME

BY
JASON LOMELINO
& THE IV CHURCH FAMILY

Sea Hill Press Inc.
Santa Barbara

Sea Hill Press Inc.
www.seahillpress.com
Santa Barbara, California
Book design by Walter Sharp

Cover photography: Bre Reed
Portrait photography: Josh Morton

ISBN: 978-1-937720-28-5

Printed in the United States of America

I want to dedicate this book to our first spiritual daughter, Annalisa Morris, whose life was radically changed one night at Jesus Burgers many years ago.

Your life of love and sacrifice has never gone unnoticed by your Father in Heaven. I don't think I could be more thankful for the woman of God you have become and the life you live for King Jesus. Thank you for being you. Know that Holly and I will always be two of your biggest fans. We love you and are honored to call you our daughter in Christ.

CONTENTS

PART 2: HOPE

PART 3: LOVE

We released the first Jesus Burgers book in 2012. Testimonies came in from all over the nation of people whose lives were encouraged and inspired by what Jesus is doing in the lives of young people today. A prison in California received a handful of books, which ended up going viral throughout the place and effecting the inmates towards transformation in their own lives. There was also a group of people, now our friends, who picked up the book at Barnes & Noble in North Carolina, who ended up getting on a plane and joining us for Jesus Burgers. Since releasing the first book, we have heard of new Jesus Burgers and similar ministries beginning in other places. With God's evident hand on the ministry, we decided to create a website to help in this process of mobilizing this movement across the nation. Feel free to check it out and watch videos, hear testimonies, and learn more about Jesus Burgers:

www.jesusburgers.org

PROLOGUE:
TURN YOUR CUP
UPSIDE DOWN

JASON LOMELINO

As you read the Jesus Burgers book, I hope you feel encouraged and inspired by all Jesus has done in the lives of those who share their stories and who testify about what Jesus is still doing today in the city of Isla Vista.

Jesus Burgers began with a simple idea to love people. We have yet to detour from that mission. Love can look like many things, but it does need to look like something. For us it's a hamburger, a kind word, maybe a prayer, or a listening ear. To me this is what every Friday night is about—being the hands and feet of Jesus, meeting people where they're at, and loving them in a tangible way.

I want to begin this book with one inspiring story—a story I only recently heard about from one of the ladies who was part of the Jesus Burgers ministry but moved to Long Beach for school. She attended a church where Lead Pastor Darren Rouanzoin gave his life to Jesus at Jesus Burgers.

Pastor Rouanzoin's story serves as a wonderful reminder of what Jesus said when describing the

Kingdom of Heaven being like a man who sowed good seed in the field. Over the years, we have sowed countless good seeds, usually not knowing what God did with them. Once in a while, you hear someone's story . . .

I moved to Santa Barbara and had just left the Christian faith. I was studying theater and planned to become a famous actor. I was eighteen-years-old and had moved from home to an off-campus apartment residence at UCSB. My roommates were partiers. One grew mushrooms under his bed, one sold drugs, and one made inappropriate movies with his girlfriend while the rest of us were out.

I had somehow managed to organize my schedule throughout the week around keg parties hosted by various fraternities and clubs: the ski and snowboard club on Tuesday, the Jewish fraternity on Thursday, the surf club on Friday, etc. There were endless possibilities for a random house party. When you live in Isla Vista, there is always a party you can go to. Girls, drugs, and alcohol were all part of a normal week at UCSB.

One fall night, I had wandered down Del Playa, the main street, while carrying a red cup full of beer. I was drinking heavily that night, masking loneliness and depression. I had been known to take my anger out on people by arguing "reverse-apologetics." I would find myself talking to Christians about their faith and arguing away their "inferior" beliefs. I recall having a few successful conversations with strangers and remembering the moment their parents' faith couldn't hold up in a real conversation while they surrounded themselves with parties and alcohol. I was convincing people to leave their faith.

But this one night, I stumbled into the front lawn

of a house that was passing out free hamburgers. As I stood there sobering up with my empty beer cup in one hand and half-eaten hamburger in another, a woman who I knew was Christian walked up to me. As she approached me, I suddenly realized I was at a Christian outreach of some sort, a house passing out free burgers—they called them Jesus Burgers.

I didn't know what to do. She walked up, and I was ready to engage, ready to argue my philosophical arguments with stellar accuracy and persuasion. The only problem was she didn't come to argue. She came to warn me, but not about eternal damnation apart from Jesus like so many other Christians might have done. Instead she said, "Turn your cup upside down."

"Turn my cup upside down?"

She said, "If the cops see you with a red cup, they will give you a ticket for drinking in public. Turn it upside down so they know there's nothing in it."

She was kind.

Suddenly, in my head and heart I heard another kind voice, not one of disappointment or insecurity, but one of possibility, "What are you doing?"

It was God.

At least that's what I thought in the moment.

I ran home.

Literally, RAN HOME.

I went into my room, fell to my knees, and confessed my sins out loud. That took a little longer than I anticipated. There were a lot of 'em.

I asked Jesus back into my life.

Right there, alone, in my drug-abusing, porn-making, party-central dorm room.

Jesus, I'm sorry.

Jesus, forgive me.

Jesus, I give my life to you.

That was it.

I stopped partying and drinking that moment.

I stopped everything.

I showed back up to the Jesus Burgers house that Sunday and a few Sundays after. It was called Isla Vista Church, and it was and is a ministry to college students in Isla Vista. I would show up to the backyard Sunday gatherings and weep.

I wept a lot.

I cried like a little baby.

I was broken.

Broken for what I did.

Broken because I had blown my witness.

I was lost. I was hurting.

A few months later, I left UCSB full of shame and guilt.

I went to a junior college and started going to church called RockHarbor.

I eventually transferred to a school called Vanguard, a private Christian school. The reasons I planned on going there were to get away from junior college and because Vanguard was close to the beach. It was a win-win. Plus, there was the unspoken excitement about a statistic at the school: there was a 4 to 1 ratio of girls to guys. There was no way a guy could leave Vanguard without some hot lady with him! (Which is true to my story; I met my wife during my second semester.)

One day when sitting in church, I heard that familiar voice again, "Lead leaders; pastor pastors," then in my own imagination I saw myself teaching next to the teaching pastor at my church at the time. I was nineteen-years-old. I was studying theater at Vanguard.

The last thing on earth I wanted to do was go into vocational ministry. I had known since I was a child I would be an actor one day. That was who I was.

4

But, following Jesus, the real Jesus, will eventually confront every false identity, every idol, and every object of worship, and invite you to choose—to choose life that is life, or some filtered, curated veneer that gives you meaning and purpose but leaves you feeling empty. The only way to live is for Jesus.

All in.

So, I went all in. After a few months of debating it, I finally said yes to Jesus and gave up my hopes and dreams of being an actor. I changed majors and decided to pursue being some kind of pastor.

After graduating college, I got hired at the church. Three months into the job, I heard that strange voice again. I was living in Newport Beach, engaged, and planning to go on a short-term mission trip to India.

"Plant a church in Long Beach."

Newport is not Long Beach.

All I knew about Long Beach was that it was the birthplace of gangsta rap and Snoop Dogg. I was a twenty-two-year-old surfer from Orange County. It didn't make sense.

But I had to do it.

So, eventually I got married to my best friend, Alexandra, and a year later we, at twenty-three- and twenty-four-years-old, moved to Long Beach to start a church in the inner city.

It has been five years, and God has truly blessed what He asked us to do.

Every time I get up to preach or talk about Jesus and his message, I can't help but think about the kid who was lost in Isla Vista and met Jesus through the kindness of a simple ministry passing out burgers to a drunk, depressed, college kid like me.

I don't know where I would be if it wasn't for Jesus Burgers. I am thankful. I am humbled.

1

FAITH

FAITH IS THE CONFIDENCE THAT WHAT WE HOPE FOR
WILL ACTUALLY HAPPEN; IT GIVES US ASSURANCE
ABOUT THINGS WE CANNOT SEE.

HEBREWS 11:1 (NLT)

HE SHATTERS
SHAME

TROY YAMASAKI

S eventeen years of perfect attendance at Sunday
school, and there I was at yet another church
camp—bitter and apathetic. Sitting during the
last worship set, I felt even more distant from God
than before I had come; my heart was too hard to
receive the life-transforming truth about the Gospel.

"Look at all these 'Christians,'" I thought indig-
nantly. "They're responding to God because He must
love them. But not me. How could God ever love a
screw-up like me?" During this stage of my life, I
listened to lies like this unceasingly, and I believed
them. After all, I had ungratefully squandered the
rich blessings of God.

I was like the prodigal son. Physically speaking, I
had it made: I grew up in a beautiful California sub-
urb, my family was consistently whole and healthy,
and I had my fair share of toys. Even spiritually,
I lacked no good thing: my parents are both born-
again believers and they raised my brother and I with
an inspired love and fervor. In spite of how much our
parents loved us, they still would always insist that
God loved us way more than they ever could. The

9

notion didn't make perfect sense to my four-year-old rationale, but I believed it.

As I aged, however, this childlike faith waned. I began to worry about what my peers thought of me, and I began to look for value according to what our culture said about me. Simultaneously, lies about God's love being proportionate to my ability to perform began to tarnish my faith. Slowly, my relationship with the living God was replaced by a counterfeit religion—one comprised of fake smiles and lengthy rituals for a distant God. My view of Jesus became obscured by the endless lists of rules to focus on. The fruit of this mindset was a lifestyle of guilt, dictated by the shame of "not doing enough" to be loved, and filled with the fear of going to hell. By high school, I had had my fill of stale morality. Like the prodigal son, I squandered my inheritance—my Christian upbringing.

I had learned to operate a dual-lifestyle: Sundays I went to church, and Wednesdays I went to youth group; but the rest of the week I did my own thing. By my sophomore year of high school, I became heavily steeped in the party scene. I didn't just participate in it, I identified with it. For a short while, I was the kid who proudly knew where all the parties were going to be. In this seemingly lofty position, I found something that vaguely resembled the acceptance I desired, and I settled for it. But the appeal of the party scene was short-lived.

The summer before my junior year, one of my close friends died of alcohol poisoning. Many of the people we had consistently partied with didn't go to his funeral. Our shallow relationships were shown for what they truly were. I was crushed; the very acceptance I had previously worked so hard to earn was now a fount of profound rejection. It turned out that our "loving" one another was nothing more than using each other in the midst of fearing our own loneliness. I had exchanged my relationship with God for a love as counterfeit as this. In fact, I myself had loved others with this selfish and fake affection. I could not believe what I had done; the guilt was potent and the self-condemnation was ever-present.

I plummeted. Whether it was through alcohol, drugs, or pornography, I desperately grasped at anything that could muffle the anger and confusion that was suffocating my mind. I fooled myself into thinking I was fine, but I had secretly begun drinking at school and had gotten into the habit of drinking myself to sleep. I wanted people to care, but I was too ashamed about my life decisions to receive any form of love. When I considered how far I had fallen, the feelings of isolation and emptiness seemed like an appropriate way to punish myself. So I hid beneath a rebellious caricature at school and continued to push away people who genuinely cared about me. I felt ashamed for hating my life. "You are so ungrateful! How dare you be depressed; you have no right to feel this way. You suck."

It was with this emaciated spirit and an incognito bottle of vodka that I went to that church camp. Return with me now to the closing worship set: I was sitting in a posture of rebellion thinking, "God must hate me," and then something baffled me.

"What is that?" my callous heart croaked. For the first time in a long time, I felt this slight tickle—as though something had gotten through my heart's crusty exterior and pricked the part of it that was still soft. I had spent the past few years of my life as the prodigal son, and now right before my very eyes I saw the Father's outstretched hand with utter clarity. It was not through the talent of the worship team or the wisdom of the speakers—I was moved by a mentally impaired individual. Both hands raised and eyes tightly shut, he was worshipping in whole-hearted sincerity. He was holding back tears, and he was singing loudly—shouting even. I don't even think he was singing the words correctly, but he didn't care! It was just him and God, and he was determined to love God extravagantly.

I could not avoid the marvelous Savior he was singing to. In that moment, the lies like "not good enough" and "worthless" had no place in this young man's heart. And I heard God singing louder than these lies, even louder than the worship. He was pro-claiming, "How deep is My love for you! You are be-loved and precious! You are My child." My notion of a god with cheap fairy-tale love was obliterated.

The event struck me profoundly. However, after I came back from the camp, nothing changed for a while. The bad habits and attitudes were stubborn, but deep down a strong sense of spiritual homesick-ness was developing. I couldn't keep running from God. During my senior year of high school, my beau-tiful and clumsy walk with Jesus began. Slowly the need to escape reality was being shaped into a life defined by the reality of the cross.

However, my heart was still more familiar with the oppression of shame than God's reign of uncon-ditional love. I was like the prodigal son who upon returning home could only recognize that he did not deserve to be his father's son ever again. But in His mighty jealousy for me, God would not relent un-til He crushed the lie that told me I didn't belong to Him. One particular summer night in 2012, God took a powerful hold of my heart. I was just driving home on the freeway, thanking God for His good-ness. Suddenly, my face started trembling and my eyes began watering uncontrollably. My whole body had chills, and a waterfall of warmth gushed from my heart. It felt like my heart had been covered in barnacles, but in that moment, a roaring wave came in and crushed them. This wave of living water decimated their ability to cling to my heart. God shattered the shame that had held me from Him for so long. I cannot really rationalize this experience, but looking back, I consider it to be the night that I was truly born again into a new life. Like a broken window that can never be restored, I felt the hand of God break my guilt before Him.

As soon as I got home that night, I blurted out to my parents, "Mom! Dad! I need a Bible!"

"Well, we have Bibles," they confusedly remarked.

"No, I really need to pick out my own Bible."

So that weekend, I went and got a brown leather, pocket-sized NIV. And it was with this precious little book that I would venture into the next chapter of my life: college.

After a lot of prayer, I followed God's call to attend UC Santa Barbara. Equally delighted and anxious, I knew it didn't make perfect sense at the time. After being recently redeemed from the party scene, I was now being called to one of the top-rated party schools in the nation. "I'll be praying for you" was the statement I heard frequently from the members of my church. Shortly after moving to Santa Barbara, however, I found myself greatly encouraged by the presence of strong Christians in UCSB's student body—I initially signed up for at least five different Christian clubs that first week! With born-again zeal, I figured that if I immersed myself in Christian community and fixed my eyes on Jesus, the whole party scene would be easily avoided. Little did I know that Jesus and an amazing community awaited me smack-dab in the middle of the party scene!

"Wait, you guys do what?!"

I listened intently as my new friend, Brendon, explained the routine, "Yea, man! Every Friday we grill up a ton of burgers on Del Playa and just give 'em to people for free."

That first night at Jesus Burgers was pretty unforgettable. It was my first night returning to the drone of techno music and intoxicated shouts. It was awkward to be back around the superficial pleasures that the party scene had to offer. But in a sea of empty lifestyle, I was at a house that offered the city something better. And it wasn't just a free burger, it was hope. It was the hope that their lives were valuable and meant to celebrate something greater. This group of young people was offering the Good News about Jesus, the hope of the nations.

Put simply: I went that first Friday, and I loved it—from pressing the burgers to grilling them, from sharing my story to listening to others, from praying over someone to cleaning up their vomit, from giving a ride to doing the dishes—and I have been going ever since. I am truly honored and stoked that God has included me in such a radical pursuit of His prodigal sons and daughters.

One night, I received a call from a friend. She was asking me to pray for her roommate; the roommate had been raped while she was out partying. It was utterly heartbreaking to hear. Later that week, I felt led to share God's compassion with this poor girl by giving her some chocolate. My close friend Jake volunteered to go buy the chocolate while I wrote her a simple note. It read: "You are beautiful/ You are valuable/ You are loved / (signed) El Roi, the God who sees your hurt."

Jake rushed over to the store and got her a Reese's

and a random Dove Cookies and Cream chocolate. We had our friend put the simple gift on her roommate's desk. Later, our friend shared how her roommate was astonished by the gift. The "random" chocolates that Jake had picked up just so happened to be her two absolute favorites! She had no idea where they could have come from; at the time she hadn't told any of her college friends what her favorite candies were. Thank You, Holy Spirit! She also had taken the note and taped it to the mirror she used every day. What a way for God to pour out true identity in her life! It is such a joy to say that no matter what's been done to us, or what we ourselves have done, God's tangible love will always make us nothing short of undone!

In the school year of 2013–14, I was privileged to call the Jesus Burgers house home. As Jason says, "The Jesus Burgers house is like a pressure cooker." While the intense atmosphere presented profound challenges, it simultaneously took my walk with Jesus to new depths of utter dependence upon His grace. And what a gnarly year it was. From a full-on riot to a shooting, reconciliation and revival proved to be a messy business. But it's right in the middle of the mess where God has called His church in Isla Vista.

As I reflect on the hardships, I cannot help but also give thanks for how powerfully God has used Jesus Burgers in the few years I've been involved. I have seen dozens cry as they encounter the love of God for the first time through prayer; I have seen people stop partying just to observe us worship in the Upper Room; I have witnessed several individuals come to know Jesus as Savior and Friend for the first time; and I have witnessed others rededicate their lives to Him. In fact, many of these brothers and sisters are now a part of Isla Vista Church and are even contributing to this book! Between the two-hundred free burgers given out every Friday and the countless number of love-filled conversations that occur, who knows how many of these seeds will make an eternal impact? If living at the Jesus Burgers house has taught me anything, it's the glorious truth that light does not flee from the darkness, but darkness flees from the light.

At the end of the day, Jesus Burgers has very little to do with the delicious burgers we give away. Jesus Burgers is about partnering with the outstretched hand of God; it's about witnessing people become never-the-same-again. Jesus Burgers is about God's people getting right up where it's the messiest and most painful and sharing the only hope that can comfort the helpless. It's about proclaiming to a city that God doesn't stay at a distance when He says, "I love you." His love is as tangible as a burger. It's about how this same Savior is very near and moving powerfully this very day.

In a place known for its reckless partying, God is creating a new reputation. Isla Vista is becoming the place where God's children are recklessly rejoicing in Him. From notorious to glorious, that's the type of party that IV was made for. That's the type of party I was made for.

A FAITHFUL FATHER

LIZZY HERNANDEZ

From a very young age, I believed God existed. Indeed, I had a child-like faith, but God was presented to me in a way that did not reveal His loving character as my Father. I was baptized in the Catholic Church as an infant, and then at the age of five, I began attending Mass and Catechism classes with my neighbor, whom I lived with, a kind woman named Randi. I asked a lot of questions during Catechism class, but no answers seemed to satisfy my curiosity. Thankfully, within a few years, Randi and I got connected to an Assembly of God community where I learned of God's goodness, began speaking in youth group, and was baptized again. This church became our family, and I came to enjoy the presence of God through prayer and reading the Bible.

The two years that I lived with Randi were a time in my childhood that I look back on and cherish. However, at age ten, tension grew between Randi and my parents as my parents wanted me back, often threatening to take me to Mexico if I did not spend more time with them. This led to a two-year court battle over who would have guardianship over me.

After many therapists, psychiatrists, mediators, and lawyers weighed in, the court did the best they could to analyze the situation and reach a final ruling on where I was to live. Throughout the battle, Randi and I simply prayed that God's will would be done, though I hoped to live with her. However, my parents and Randi still could not reach an agreement. So, after two more years, I was sent to live with my parents.

Before long my father lost his job. We were forced to relocate for his new job, and I finished the eighth grade having experienced for the first time heavy waves of loneliness and depression. The summer before my first year of high school began, my big brother passed away from a fatal seizure, and my parents lost their house. This drew my family closer. We could not understand why my brother was taken from us at such a young age, and we needed each other to get through such horrific times. Whatever relationship I had with God was lost because I could not understand why He would allow such traumatic events to happen and why He would take such meaningful people as Randi and my brother out of my life.

Eventually, I stopped caring about myself and others and developed an apathetic attitude as a way of coping. Living with my parents was difficult. I did not respect them, so I would rebel against them, constantly causing heated arguments between us. The loneliness I felt living with my parents never left, and depression would come and go. It was in those times I remember praying that God would rescue me from these feelings. Nonetheless, I was angry with Him and was unsure if He even heard my prayers.

Finally, I was off to college and beyond excited to escape all of these problems. However, I quickly realized that those awful feelings from before would not leave me simply because I had moved. I joined the Ultimate Frisbee team and got in with a crowd that really enjoyed drinking, so I started drinking and smoking marijuana in excessive amounts. With every shot, I drowned my loneliness and frustration, usually ending the night blacked out and puking, knowing my friends would fill me in on the shameful things I said or did in the morning. My reputation of being wild was all too humorous to me, but I also tried to deny it because, in my heart, that was not the real me. I felt so incredibly lost.

Spring quarter I fell into a spell of depression that left me desperate to escape the feeling that something was wrong with me and missing from my life. Conversations with friends were about alcohol, parties, and boys, but they only left me feeling emptier and more alone. I also felt incredibly unintelligent as I fell behind in classes and failed midterms due to poor study habits. By the grace of God, I managed to pass every class. My last day of freshmen year ended in a haze as I was so high on marijuana that I could not tell if what was happening was real or not. This continued on into the summer and got to the the point where my disappointed father caught me and pleaded with me to change my ways.

When I returned to Isla Vista for the following school year, my use of substances had only worsened, but I decided to start attending a Bible study led by a friend of mine. Every time I went, I would feel guilt in my heart. I knew that either I had to choose God or choose my lifestyle. Still, I continued the cycle of drinking and then wondering why I chose to drink so much again. Alcohol was consuming me instead of it consuming my problems, and this became more and more clear as I pummeled down my dark hole of meaninglessness. I really tried to stop drinking, but I would fall right back into it the next weekend. I could not seem to pull myself out of the hole I had dug, but I wasn't yet ready to give it all to the Father.

Fall quarter I became friends with Amanda Olson, right around the time she had given her life to Jesus. She was quickly becoming a part of my life, and I would ask her many questions about God, some of which she could not answer. Her zeal for the Lord was so real, so raw, and I was truly encouraged by her faith. Indeed, the timing of our friendship felt divine as we both needed a sister for encouragement while we figured things out together. She had recently joined IV Church and would regularly invite me to Jesus Burgers, but I chose instead to party. Finally, after one last drunken, disastrous night that left me full of shame, I decided to go to Jesus Burgers with her.

There I was, soberly conversing with people, feeling like half of me was for God and the other half was still stuck in worldly ways, not ready to change. It was odd observing drunk kids trek past me when just the night before I had been in the same position as them. The night was concluding, and as I sat around the fire engaging in conversation about God and life, one of the girls who lived at the Jesus Burgers house began to jump on tables and proclaim her praise to the Lord—how He set her free and changed her life! I thought to myself, "If God is a little crazy and spontaneous like that, then I am all in." Sure enough, the night spent there would begin my walk with God.

Another one of the girls who lived at the Jesus Burgers house asked me to share with her what my childhood was like, and so I told her everything about my life up until that point. I told her of my inability to quit drinking, my struggle with marijuana, and my attempts at half-heartedly living for God. She read to me a passage from Romans 7:

"I do not understand what I do. For what I want to do I do not do, but what I hate I do. And if I do what I do not want to do, I agree that the law is good. As it is, it is no longer I myself who do it, but it is sin living in me . . . For in my inner being I delight in God's law; but I see another law at work in me, waging war against the law of my mind and making me a prisoner of the law of sin at work within me . . . Thanks be to God, who delivers me through Jesus Christ our Lord! So then, I myself in my mind am a slave to God's law, but in my sinful nature a slave to the law of sin" (NLT).

I was astonished that this was in the Bible, as this verse explained the very reason I could not stop drinking, and I ended up fully dedicating my life to God that night. I was no longer bound by my sin, as He instantly changed my desires, and instead I experienced the freedom and goodness that comes with living for the Father. I was rescued from the depths of my downward spiral, and God changed my perspective on life. Since that night, He has given me drive, direction, and love for others and myself. He has restored my relationship with my parents, and I have forgiven them of the hurt they caused me as a child. Indeed, He has filled me with hope.

Through serving at Jesus Burgers I have witnessed people's perspectives on life change as mine has. I have seen hearts soften and open to hearing about our Creator. There is one particular night that remains with me: the Friday before Deltopia. I was gathered around the bonfire with ten young men and women, most of whom I did not know. We were all gathered together discussing the depths and intricacies of what it means to believe in God, to have faith, all while listening to each other's views in such a respectful way. The non-Christians had all sorts of questions, and we even discussed my favorite topic: world religions. Buddhism came up, and I was able to give a new perspective on the religion, while one of the Jesus Burgers guys described what it means to be Christian and how selfless it is to be a servant of God. Somewhere in the conversation, a girl suggested we all go around in a circle and share what we are thankful for. People stated how thankful they were for their friends and family and for each other. One guy was thankful for all the differences we had and that we could all maturely talk about such topics. One girl was thankful for open-mindedness, and another guy was thankful for thankfulness itself. I shared how thankful I was for living in Isla Vista and having met the people around the firepit, because these led me to a conversation with fellow young people from my generation, which I am proud to be part of. Eventually, the night came to an end, and our new friends departed with grateful hearts and a conversation I hope they remember. Indeed, a seed was planted.

I am so grateful for the Jesus Burgers house. I have realized that it is truly pride that causes us to live life for ourselves. I just want to humbly serve my Father and experience Him more than ever before. His love is so sweet, so just, and so good. He was always with me—there for me in the times I would pray, there when I felt alone, and here for me now as I have chosen to live for Him again. He is truly a faithful Father, true to His word, and all it takes is believing what He says is true. People have come in and out of my life. The impermanence of people hurts my soul, but my Father above never left me, and I am comforted in the fact that He never will.

THE LOST SON

ETHAN DAVIS

I remember it being Halloween, and the crowd was around 7,500. My friend and I were the last EDM group to play that night, and as I walked onto the stage, I couldn't help but reflect on my life. All I could hear was screaming, but my head flooded with memories of the first time I picked up drumsticks, understood chords on a guitar, and learned how to play a song on the piano. Music played such a large role in my life leading up to that moment, but sadly, none of those memories impacted me the way I expected them to. As I thought about these experiences and looked out at the crowd, I expected to feel some sense of accomplishment or even satisfaction. But I didn't find it that night, or any other night during the national tour. Even though I had found myself in the music industry, a place I had fought to be for so long, it felt . . . empty.

And looking back, many areas in my life felt empty. I had mastered, or attempted to master, leading a "double life"—having one foot in and one foot out with God. As I failed to let God into every area of my life on a daily basis, the pervasive feelings of emptiness and loneliness followed close behind. I had identified myself as a Christian ever since I was introduced to Jesus at a summer camp in seventh grade, but unfortunately that didn't change my lifestyle. I know I had the head knowledge of Christianity, but I lacked the heart knowledge of what walking out a relationship with Jesus really meant. There was a separation between the two that I couldn't seem to reconcile in my own life.

By eighth grade I was drinking and smoking. Girls came on my radar, and being liked and accepted became more important than making the "right" decisions. Although I could feel the tension within myself as I delved deeper into this lifestyle, I chose to ignore the disparities and to enjoy what the world had to offer. I had a hard time associating "cool" with being a Christian. I separated the Ethan who went to church every Sunday, met up with a mentor, and hung out at church events with the Ethan who found more fulfillment in girls, parties, drugs, and alcohol.

I felt as though my life was consistently being fought for in a tug-of-war from the ages of twelve to nineteen. I held onto a lot in my life that prevented God from entirely cleaning house and giving me a fresh perspective on the actual purpose and meaning of my existence. I didn't grasp that a relationship with Jesus would give me the deepest understanding of who I was and why I was alive. I carried a legalistic mindset, believing that Christianity was a lot of rules and expectations that if failed distanced one from God. I felt distant from God, and frankly, the idea of getting close to Him didn't seem all that exciting. From my legalistic perspective, Christianity seemed to offer only so much. I often felt like I was trying to please God rather than being truly changed by Jesus's love and acceptance for my life.

It should come as no surprise that in high school I continued to struggle with purity, integrity, sobriety, and identity in Christ. These struggles slowly ate away at my ability to see things clearly and to take ownership of where my life was headed at that time. I remember convincing myself that many of the poor choices I was making in high school were fun and that I was doing what every other kid my age was doing—and that somehow made it okay. It was during this time that I hid behind my music and ability to make people laugh. It became clear to me that everyone enjoyed music and laughter, and in providing those two things I could coast through life without much intentionality or effort. I had a lot of friends on a surface level, but I never felt connected to anyone or anything consistently—including God.

So I sought refuge in music. Music was a medium that had brought me so close to God at certain points in my life and pulled me so far from God in darker moments. Either way, it became a place I could get lost in whenever I needed to disappear, escape reality, and detach myself from the double-minded life I was living. Making music was the only way I knew how to express myself. As I would get lost in creating a song for hours upon hours, it would help me cope with the loneliness I struggled with. It was therapeutic for me as it numbed a lot of the feelings I didn't know how to address or manage myself.

After high school, my focus on making music grew quickly, and I soon found a lot of my identity in it. It served to define who I was and helped me make a name for myself. Music was something I could create and then give people, a piece of me that they could relate to. I saw it as a way for me to get a message across and to do it on a larger scale. It was at this time that I found myself becoming increasingly fixated on making a career and a life out of it.

My freshman year of college, I formed an EDM group with my friend. We soon started getting recognition for the music I was producing. In a short amount of time, we got a manager, began playing shows, and started getting paid. Shortly after, I dropped out of college to pursue my music career and struggled to prioritize my walk with God. The recognition, money, and speed at which everything was happening felt exhilarating, and I still viewed Christianity as seemingly boring and mundane. I still made an effort to hold onto God through the process, and I decided at one point to stop drinking and smoking, assuming that would be taking a step in the right direction. My girlfriend helped me make those positive decisions. I was able to stick to them for a year and a half, but the reality is that simply cutting certain substances was not my solution.

Despite my efforts, I had yet to actually face and conquer my demons. I just kept myself distracted from that empty feeling I kept experiencing, even though I finally gained a lot of what I thought I wanted. I often fooled myself into thinking I could handle everything that was taking place around me. During tour, the lifestyle I was surrounding myself with did nothing but tempt me into making poor choices. The people I found myself consistently hanging out with didn't challenge me in the right ways. During a tour I was away on, my girlfriend and I broke up, and my sobriety ended that night.

I hit rock bottom when I found myself in a blacked-out drunken stupor on a stage, screaming the wrong city to the audience in the mic, then proceeding to fight with my group member during our show. I got a call from my family telling me it was time to come home. I felt the call from God, too, and I agreed, as did everyone else on tour, that it would be best for me to take some time to get my life in order.

I came home feeling pretty defeated and knowing that I had put God on the back burner. I wanted more for my life, and I knew deep down that the only way to truly clean my life up was through God. I remembered visiting the Jesus Burgers house a handful of times during my freshman year of college, and what intrigued me about the people who lived there was their excitement and genuine authentic love for Jesus; I had never seen anything like it.

I came on Friday nights, when the people from the church would grill hundreds of burgers for the students roaming the streets, many of whom were drunk and high. During these nights, I observed a lot of compassion and unconditional love for these students. It was refreshing to me. I remember watching people's lives touched by kindness, prayer, and simple conversations. It was a new way of living for Jesus that looked effortless and anything but mundane.

I remember one Friday night, when my bandmate came to Jesus Burgers and decided to bring some friends. One of the friends started having a really bad anxiety attack. Someone from Jesus Burgers ended up praying for him, and he immediately felt peace wash over him and the panic attack ended.

He came rushing over to us in awe and said, "I was having a panic attack, and they prayed for me, and it just went away!" It may not seem like a big miracle, but now anytime that guy has an anxiety attack, he will remember that night and how God healed him! I love when nonbelievers experience God in such a tangible way.

When I finally came back from tour, I decided to stick around and hang out with some of the people I had met in this community. Mac Montgomery was one of the people I ended up hitting it off with because we both had a love and passion for making music. I kept coming around to IVC, and I noticed that the way they were worshiping God felt different. There was something tangible and real about the sound that I had never experienced before, and it drew me into frequenting the Sunday service. God started revealing a lot in my heart during this time as well. I guess you could say I finally gave God the chance to clean house and rid me of a lot of harmful mindsets and lies I had believed for so long. And the more I talked about music with Mac and others, the more interested I was in how their lives had been changed by God and how they seemed satisfied and full of Jesus.

The pastor also gave messages on Sundays that spoke to me heavily, and God began to unfold the revelation of being a son. Being a son meant learning that I could always return home to my Father and experience unconditional love and acceptance. There I was, surrounded by a bunch of Christians, but this time around I noticed that the legalistic mindset I had of striving, shame, and guilt was fading away, and I didn't see this lifestyle as boring anymore. I started to grasp what it meant to have a personal relationship with Jesus, and this altered the way I saw the music, money, women, alcohol, and fame. For the first time in my life, I began to see consistency in my walk with Jesus—I was no longer one foot in, one foot out. At one point, a spot opened up at the Jesus Burgers house; by a miracle, I ended up living there.

The process was gradual, but as God transformed a lot of the mindsets I had on life, I began to notice my value for family, friendships, community, and identity in Christ growing. I made some decisions to change the trajectory that my music career was headed in, knowing that God was guiding me and helping me make some much-needed changes throughout the process. I still make music, but I don't feel empty anymore when I stare out at an audience from the stage. I now know that my worth, identity, or even success does not depend on my music. It rests in knowing that God unconditionally loves and accepts me and that He calls me His son. I feel such peace and rest from that knowledge, and I thank God for fighting for my soul during my darker hours. If He hadn't kept pursuing me even when I rejected Him, I don't know where I would be today.

God fills me. As I continue to find peace in that truth, I hope that I will be able to share that message with others. Whether it's through my music, ministry, or simple conversations, I hope that others are able to experience the joy and love I've found in Him.

Jesus + Burgers

NOT JUST
A NORMAL
MAN

MATTHEW PEVARNIK

True Christianity is different. It is not like the world in what it says, what it does, and what it believes. As people see believers living differently from the world, they will get a glimpse of who Jesus really is. They will see that Jesus was not just a normal man, but that He is much, much more than this. And as Jesus is lifted up like this, meaningless lives will be given meaning, and hope will come to the hopeless. As believers unite together and re-present Jesus to this world, we will begin to see our cities transformed one person at a time.

In my whole life, I never met a Christian. Sure, I grew up going to church, and all of my friends went to church, but I never met a Christian. I never met someone who actually believed what the Bible had to say and lived like it was true. As a result, combined with my own sinfulness, I knew Christianity wasn't true. I just didn't have a good excuse to get out of it. I finally found my excuse when I got to high school and studied evolution in my AP Biology class. I quickly devoured the material and was relieved to finally be able to dismiss those happy "Christians" and all of

Christianity. I also devoured fictional books like *The Da Vinci Code*. I liked that book in particular because it turned Jesus into just a normal man. However, it was the revelation that Jesus is not just a normal man that led me to the cross years later.

By the time I entered college, I was a self-proclaimed atheist and was always searching for something. I tried everything I could think of to find contentment and purpose. I started this search in middle school with doing so much math that I took the hardest AP Calculus class as a freshman in high school. I looked also to music and played the French horn for seven years, eventually playing in semi-professional orchestras. I then looked to science and worked at the prestigious international physics hub of CERN. At one point in my life, I did not spend a day sober for two years straight. Everything I could think of doing that was praiseworthy and meaningful had just left me empty and dissatisfied. I was ready to give up hope in this world.

At UC Irvine, where I was pursuing a PhD in physics, a girl came up to me in Jamba Juice and asked me if I was interested in Bible study. I snapped back, "BIBLE study!?! Why would you ask me that??"

She replied back with a smile on her face, "Oh, I'm asking everybody today . . . so . . . would you like to?"

I thought "Well, she's kind of cute, and honestly, I have never taken a look at the Bible," so I agreed to meet up the following week.

When I first sat down with this girl, little did I know that my life was about to change forever. I quickly found out that I was not sitting down with some Christian girl who wavered in her faith and, as I hoped, was not interested in getting in a relationship with me, the atheist. Instead, I was sitting down with a fiery girl who wanted nothing more than to see people come into the Kingdom of God. I was immediately amazed when she talked about Jesus because she talked about Jesus, as if she actually knew Him. I had never met a Christian who genuinely loved God like this. She actually believed what the Bible had to say and had a testimony to back it up! Little did I know how much she would affect my life.

A couple of months later, she invited me to a conference her church was hosting. At this conference, we did a Bible study on the crucifixion of Jesus from Luke 23. My whole world was turned upside down as I saw this man, Jesus, respond unlike any man I had ever met. I couldn't think of anyone in the whole world who would ever respond like Jesus did to those who were murdering Him. He simply prayed things like, "Father, forgive them, for they know not what they do," and He didn't justify Himself despite their threats, accusations, and insults. In this moment, I knew that He was not just a normal man.

The following morning, my friend shared her testimony along with a message on the Parable of the Prodigal Son (Luke 15:11–32). I quickly saw that my life was like that of the prodigal son. I felt so ashamed of where my life had ended up, and I wanted something more, something different. I began weeping as I saw the unstoppable love of the Father come running towards His wayward son. In the twinkling of an eye, Christianity made sense to me. Though I was that wayward son, Jesus had died in my place on the cross, and my sin could not stop the Father from pouring His love out upon me. I didn't understand what just happened, but something changed permanently within me. I felt a real sense of purpose and hope that I had never experienced before. I returned to UC Irvine as a new man.

After encountering the Living God, I decided that I wanted to grow faster than any disciple ever had before. Though terrified of the thought of evangelism, I knew that other people had to know who Jesus really was. I was like the Samaritan woman at the well in John 4, who went and told her whole village about the Messiah, despite being a Christian for only a few hours! Looking back, it is amazing that someone who had never read more than a few chapters of the Bible could share such stupendous truths about Jesus. Though I did have a passion to know everything the Bible had to say, this is not what qualified me to share about Jesus. What qualified me to talk about Jesus was that I had met Him, knew Him, and was growing to know Him more. After a year of this lifestyle, I married that fiery girl, Victoria, and we embarked on a wild journey together with Jesus. It is impossible to not have adventures when married to someone who loves Jesus more than life itself. Little did we know that just over two years later, we would end up living in a wild little town called Isla Vista and giving birth to a baby girl named Hope right after arriving there.

Moving to a new area, we immediately went looking for a church body to plug into. We went to Isla Vista Church's Sunday gathering. During the time of worship, my heart broke for the people in that church and for the city. I wept over people I had never even met, but I felt there was such hope and grace ready to be poured out for each and every person in Isla Vista. I knew this was where God wanted us, since after service my wife began describing how during worship she saw a vision of the city and began weeping over it at the exact same time I wept for this place. We experienced the tiniest fraction of the love that the Father has for this city, and it was overwhelming. His love cannot be quenched, even though the city's inhabitants may have feet that are swift to do evil. He is committed to raising up people to share His love with Isla Vista.

At Jesus Burgers, I quickly saw a fresh perspective of the freedom in Christ that we have. I saw believers doing many different things. Some Christians were at the grill, either making burgers or talking to people in the line. Other Christians were inside of the Jesus Burgers house talking to partiers, giving them water, a bathroom, or a place to escape the party scene. Others were in the back making intercession for the ministry. Finally, another group took to the streets and stood by a "Free Blessings" sign or walked up and down amongst the people. There was not one set way to do Evangelism, but rather many creative ways where people were able to show kindness to a city in a way unique to them as individuals. Thus, with me, the PhD scientist and Jesus lover, I tended to end up in very intellectual conversations, running into every argument (or excuse) that an atheist can make.

I learned that no Christian ought ever be intimidated by the most well-versed of atheists, whether they are professors of science, archaeology, history, or just regular partygoers. It's easy to defend something that's true, as every method to observe it will yield information in favor of that truth. Anything that seems contradictory to Truth will ultimately prove to be false. But, these facts are generally not what I've found opens up hearts to allowing the seed of life to enter in. Yes, they are great to know and can be useful in a pinch, but this is not what has opened up the people I've encountered in Isla Vista to the Gospel.

One evening as I was walking up and down the streets praying in my mind for people, the spirit of God immediately drew me to this one group of guys. We started a conversation, and I found out that they were all skeptics, or at least skeptical about Christianity. One gentleman and I went back and forth for about thirty minutes. He seemed to know all the best objections to Christianity, and I knew all of the responses to those common objections.

After about thirty minutes, he stopped me and said, "You know what. This is amazing. I have cut you off from speaking at least twenty times, and you just let me speak. If I were you, I would have said #$!*#@ so many times by now. You are something else."

It's that easy! This is a seed of the Kingdom planted not through the clever words of man, but through the gentle ear of a listening believer. Four months later, as I was returning from Jesus Burgers another evening, I saw the same gentleman standing in the middle of the street by my house. He was lost (physically that is), but upon seeing me, he greeted me like a long lost friend.

He was so happy that he blurted out, "Woah! It's you! This is so amazing! I can't believe it's you! This has got to be . . ." and then he paused.

He was afraid to finish, so my wife helped him out, " . . . God," she said.

And he said "Yeah, God!"

This man is a picture of a generation wandering in the streets, lost in a sea of meaninglessness and emptiness, but the Father is always looking. He is always searching for the one lost sheep. He doesn't need Christians who are eloquent in speech, or who know every fact about the Bible, archeology, geology, physics, or biology. He needs believers who spend time with Him, ready to love and be kind to this world. Through this love and kindness, the world will start to see that Jesus is not just a normal man. They will be strangely drawn to this man, the Son of God, and ultimately, into the Kingdom of God.

FREE
AT LAST

MARISSA HOWARD

I'm tempted not to talk at all about my life before I met Jesus. That person is no longer me—to the point where I don't recognize her anymore. I don't dwell on the past or live in past pain. In fact, I am a firm believer that your circumstances do not define who you are. And looking back on that girl, I could cry for her. I see that girl in so many faces walking through the streets here in Isla Vista. I think it's important to understand the person I was, in order to comprehend how God helped destroy my noxious ideas of life, helped restore me, and transformed me completely.

I could tell you about the abuse and toxic relationships, the lies I told to friends and family, the innocence that was taken from me way too young, and the following struggle to prove that I had control over the men I put in my life, I used to believe that in order for a man to love me he needed to abuse me in some way, or that it was my job to "fix" him. Physically and emotionally I would let men control my life and allow them to guide my actions. I craved the acceptance of people and took pride in my ability

37

to woo and manipulate everyone I crossed paths with. I was engrossed with a lifestyle of being the life of the party and always pretended I had everything together. I was a free spirit, crazy, spontaneous, and the girl "your kids shouldn't hang around." I grew up way too fast and would take off in a sprint from any situation or person who expressed they wanted to control me, make a commitment to me, or try and tie me down in any way. What was the use of trying to preserve something that had already been taken away from me?

I was rebellious and angry. I chain-smoked, drank, and danced on tables. My story mimicked the ones I heard growing up in church of people being saved from a life of sex and drugs. I never believed that story would be for me. While my life did change in a radical way, it did not happen over night. God used incredible friends and family to surround me and teach me what His love was really all about.

At the age of sixteen, after finishing my sophomore year of high school, I boarded a plane to California with a one-way ticket and plans to start over. I knew I was never going to change in my little town of Bethel, Connecticut, so I made my way to Redding, California, where family took me in. I had no idea that this city and the culture they cultivated there would change my life. I found myself at a Jesus Culture concert and, imitating the people around me, I held my hands up in the air. With worship led by Kim Walker, I had a radical encounter with the Holy Spirit. I could feel my body become light, and the burdens I carried were lifted off of me. People prophesied over my life and told me the incredible plan God had for me and my future. I began to believe them. Following a long sequence of events, brave communication, and people who refused to give up on me, I became someone who knew how to love herself and find joy in every aspect of my life. After a year of restoration, I decided to attend Bethel School of Ministry.

Two years there changed my entire life and shaped me into the passionate woman I am today. I was changed by a love encounter with God. I was no longer mad at the world, myself, or my circumstances. I trusted God to take care of them, and I was going to focus on being happy. I pursued my passion for travel—hopping on planes all over the world and watching God work through me to bring joy, love, healing, and prophecy to prostitutes, sex slaves, the poorest of the poor, churches seeking change, and ordinary people. God gave me wisdom to speak to all kinds of people and listen to their stories and love them exactly where they were, the same way people did for me. In my time at Bethel, I met my incredible husband who has championed me in every way, supports my dreams, and loves me unconditionally. Our strengths compliment one another so well, and with his desire to see people healed and mine to love and prophesy, we are an amazing team. Jeremy sees the best in me and I in him, and my life with Jesus and him is significant, purposeful, and happy.

My focus, however, is not how crazy my life was before I met Jesus, but how exhilarating it has become with Him now. I've never done anything conventional my entire life. Every decision and event that has happened has always been completely out of the ordinary, and God has poured favor into so many areas of my life. He has shown me how many times throughout my life He has been there for me. And my goal everyday is to help one other person realize that they are allowed to be happy, they are loved, and they are known. I've seen a blind man be given his sight, a woman break down crying because God had shown me her deepest secrets, broken bones be healed, tumors disappear, and people experience God's tangible presence. It is something that can't be ignored; you can't hide from the love of God.

While I no longer live in the past, and rarely discuss the terrified little girl who once encompassed me, I am able to use my testimony to show people that God can grab hold of your life and give you the miracle of faith. He will romance you, extinguish your fear, and give you the audacity to take the fragile, weak, broken things in your life and conquer them until your life is submerged with only the exceptional.

My life is filled with the joy and love of God. I would have thought that was utterly ridiculous years ago. I didn't believe God could "save" people. I believed it was all a hoax, a way to get people to behave. I realized my rooted rebellious attitude could be applied to something much more incredible. It was crazy to approach people and pray for them, especially to see healing in their bodies. How could I be skeptical when things were happening before my eyes?

Life with Jeremy has been an adventure from the start. After praying, prophesying, healing the sick, and loving on people together, we knew that was what we were called to do. Whether it was grocery shopping, on a date, road tripping, or at church, we were prepared to share what God had in store for the people around us. Now that we call Isla Vista — one of the craziest college party towns there is — our home, there is opportunity for ministry all around us (including the people who live behind us that set off fireworks at three o'clock in the morning).

We made our move to Isla Vista two years ago, after a ministry trip over Halloween weekend. The trip was filled with prophetic words and a love connection with the church. Living in Isla Vista as a young married couple is definitely not normal and a little strange, but we were sure that was where God wanted us. Our second year, Jeremy led the Upper Room, which opened a lot of doors for us to speak into people's lives. Investing in the people of our church and the people partying on the streets has accumulated a ton of testimonies of healing and love in our city.

One of my favorite testimonies was on Friday night, late into the evening, about one o'clock, sitting down with a girl eating her Jesus Burgers hamburger on the front lawn of the Jesus Burgers house. I immediately connected with her. I saw the pain in her dilated pupils, her exposed skin on a chilly winter evening, with sweat on her forehead, her teeth grinding not from the cold but as an effect of using a drug I had once been familiar with. I sat down with her and began to ask her a few questions about herself.

She was feeling anxious and nauseous and would often suddenly be confused. She didn't understand why someone would want to know anything about her. She began to tell me her life story, filled with divorce, abuse, and heartbreak. I listened for over an hour while she cried, and I cried with her. I told her that she was a daughter of the best Father ever and loved deeper than she could ever comprehend. Her tears poured as I spoke life into her and called out who she was supposed to be. I shared with her how I came to Jesus and how my life is radically different than it once was. I asked if I could pray for her, and she said yes. I first prayed for the bad symptoms of drug use to disappear, and she immediately sobered up. I remember her looking up at me and telling me the weight she had been feeling over her entire body had lifted. Her anxiety visibly disappeared and her teeth stopped grinding. She told me she wanted to experience the same thing I had. That night she allowed me to pray, and she accepted the love of God into her heart. All it takes is one experience for your life to be changed forever.

Being surrounded by an incredible family that loves so well at Isla Vista Church has changed my view of family altogether. Isla Vista reminds me every day that restoration and transformation is for everyone. "Therefore if any man be in Christ, he is a new creature: old things are passed away; behold, all things are become new" (2 Corinthians 5:17). You are made NEW! God does not keep any record of your wrongs! You are clean in his eyes. You are his precious sons and daughters! Having an understanding of this can wreck your life forever! Ephesians 4:22–24 says,

"You were taught, with regard to your former way of life, to put off your old self, which is being corrupted by its deceitful desires; to be made new in the attitude of your minds; and to put on the new self, created to be like God in true righteousness and holiness."

I am determined to fight for lost hearts and cover people with grace. I want to come alongside them and bring them into their true identity, starting here in Isla Vista. I am called to bring justice to a world that needs hope and bring it through a heavenly perspective. I have found the freedom I was rebelling for my entire life.

I am someone who has found love. Inconvenient, unconventional, ridiculous, influential, consuming, inspiring, infuriating, unconditional love. And in this love and joy I found, I have never been more free.

COLLIDING
OF HEAVEN
AND EARTH

JEREMY HOWARD

Most kids have grandiose dreams of becoming superheroes, astronauts, or professional athletes, but at some point in their lives are told to grow up and aim for something more realistic. That was something I could never do.

I've always believed I was destined to do something significant. My dream since I was five-years-old was to play professional baseball. My whole life revolved around baseball, so much so that at sixteen-years-old my whole family moved from Montana to California so I could play year round and hopefully get enough exposure to get a Division 1 college scholarship. The move ended up leading to many offers from small schools, but none from the schools I wanted to go to. I almost ended up at the University of San Francisco, but I realized my family wasn't able to afford the tuition costs, and I reluctantly decided to go play JUCO baseball in Santa Barbara, California. To this day I still wonder if this was the best decision or worst decision of my college career. I had the worst year of baseball I'd ever had in my life and, to be honest, didn't make many friends. Along with the sports and social problems, I was trying to figure out who God was or if He even existed.

I grew up in a Christian family and at thirteen-years-old made a personal commitment to serve God, even though I didn't really know what it was supposed to look like. If you aren't familiar with the sports world (or religion for that matter) you should know everything is performance based. Everywhere you go you play to get the approval of your coach, college/pro scouts, fans, your teammates, and unfortunately at times your own parents and family. Not only does the world of athletics say you need to perform at a certain level for acceptance, but religion does as well. Living with this mindset of performing for approval carried over into my relationship with God. I found myself exhausted, continually trying to keep all my junk together so God would be okay with me. Every day was difficult, but it seemed like that was the way it was supposed to be. Many other Christians I talked with all seemed to have a rough time and were just continuing to "persevere" and "continue in faith" until Jesus comes back. I always felt like something was missing but could never figure out what it was. I saw the lifestyle of my teammates—drinking, partying, and hooking up with as many girls as they could—and I knew what I wanted deep in my heart wasn't in that. Yet at the same time I knew I didn't have what Jesus called "life abundantly."

After a long year in Santa Barbara, I moved back home to San Jose and decided to take a year off baseball, the hardest decision of my life. Once baseball wasn't in the picture, I didn't know what to do with my life. My whole identity and everything about me was linked to baseball. I had never imagined doing anything but baseball. Thus, I began the journey of learning who I was outside of baseball.

I decided to help out with my high school youth group at church just to keep myself busy while I figured out what I wanted to do with my life. What I soon realized was that God had set me up with some of the most loving people I'd ever met. For the first time in my life I was around people who didn't need me to perform for them; I was accepted when I walked in the door. It took me awhile to realize I didn't have to try and act cool to fit in. What I learned was that these people had a different view of God; they knew Him as a loving and forgiving Father, a foreign concept to me. During a dinner out, I remember asking my buddy Joe how many people he had seen "saved"; his answer: "Over one hundred."

At this point in my life I had tried to "share" Jesus with teammates and family and had never seen anyone even contemplate living for Him. I asked him how he shared the Gospel with people, and he simply said, "I just tell them about Jesus." I really didn't believe that that was all he did, but he assured me people really did want to know the real Jesus.

During this same conversation, they told me of one of their friends who had been to this school where they taught people to hear God's voice and that God was healing people of all kinds of sickness there. I met up with their friend, Martha, and was completely wrecked (in a good way) hearing all her stories of God healing people not only in churches but also out on the streets. I joke with her now that the day we met was the day I really got saved because from that conversation forward I began to meet the God I read about in the Bible. In a real and tangible way God infiltrated my life and began to show me that He had always loved me and believed in me and that there was excitement and supernatural adventure in a relationship with Him. I was finally free of performing for His love!

I ended up at Bethel School of Supernatural Ministry in Redding, California, the same school my friend Martha had been to. It was during my time there that I heard of Jesus Burgers. A year and a half into school I was engaged and again wondering where to go next. My fiancée (now wife) and I felt God had big plans for Santa Barbara, and we decided at the end of our second year we would get married and move there to partner with God's plans. We didn't have any connections in Santa Barbara, but during our second year of school we saw there was a ministry trip planned to go to Santa Barbara. We joined the team and came down on Halloween to be a part of this outreach called Jesus Burgers. Immediately, we were set on being part of Isla Vista Church. We now have countless stories of God's goodness in this small, crazy city.

It's wild to think that five years ago I was in this same city drowning in religion and wondering who I was and if God even existed. Now I'm more alive than I've ever been, and I am able to have an impact on the people around me through the Holy Spirit. Not just through simple acts of kindness, but with power. Whether it's seeing the sick healed or giving someone a prophetic word, God is releasing His love through the power of His Spirit.

You can see in people's eyes the longing for acceptance and significance as they walk the streets of IV. College is a time when people are trying to figure out who they are, and we have the opportunity to inject the love and purpose of God into their lives. I've had the craziest encounters with people who come for a hamburger at Jesus Burgers.

I love to see the power of God on display—the colliding of heaven and earth always leaves me in awe—but sometimes the simplest act can be the most profound. Right across the street from Jesus Burgers we have a sign that reads "Free Blessings." It's similar to one of those bug lights you hang outside, people find themselves wandering up sometimes not knowing what to expect, and then . . . Bam! God touches them with His goodness.

During one Friday night this guy named Rocco stood next to us staring into the street not knowing God was after his heart. We approached him and began a conversation with him. After a bit of small talk we asked if we could pray for him. He said he didn't need to be prayed for, but he quickly began to ask some deep, thought-provoking questions. It's amazing to me how much is going on underneath the surface of people. It's easy to write people off as not wanting anything to do with God, but in reality there's a deep question inside of every person who doesn't know Him intimately, and it is simply, "What is God like?"

Our conversation went on for over two hours. It was mostly me listening and him externally processing, but I could see the difference in his view of God changing as he continued to talk with us about certain experiences he'd had. He shared one story of visiting St. Peter's Basilica in Vatican City, where he began to uncontrollably weep after seeing a statue of Jesus crucified on the cross. He told us that in his head he kept thinking, why am I crying? No matter what he did he couldn't stop from crying. He ended up running out of the church with no explanation. He seemed to doubt the experience, but as we shared testimonies of our own encounters with the presence of God, he began to realize he'd had an encounter with the Holy Spirit. At the beginning of our conversation he'd said he didn't know if God was really "out there." But two hours later he was wide eyed and realizing that God had been chasing him down long before he even had a grid to comprehend an encounter with Him. Rocco didn't give his life to Jesus that night, at least not publicly, but he did realize that God wanted him and that he was loved. For a few weeks after that, Rocco would come to the Jesus Burgers house and ask others if I was around just so we could talk. We eventually exchanged phone numbers, but we never met up intentionally. But for a few weeks I would randomly see him around town, and a couple times even at my work. We would talk there, and he always expressed how much that night meant to him.

I think sometimes we can get so caught up on winning souls that we forget to love people. It's not our job to coax people into saying a prayer to go to Heaven; it's our job to demonstrate who the Father is. Jesus said, "This is eternal life, that they may know You, the only true God, and Jesus Christ whom you have sent" (John 17:3). Heaven's focus is on relationship. If we can show people the acceptance and love of the Father, people will come running into the Kingdom.

God Has
a Plan

Sam Kim

Growing up as a pastor's son, I could count on one hand the number of times I missed a Sunday service before I started college. I experienced what most pastors' kids of small Korean churches experienced: the rigid structure of Christianity without the substance.

I dreaded Sunday service in my youth because I had to wake up at seven-thirty every Sunday to help prepare for the nine o'clock service. My dad's congregation count hovered around twenty to thirty members with a majority of them aged thirty and over, which means that there was no youth group. My brother and I had to sit through pure Korean adult services. It was the same every Sunday morning. I recited prayers, sang Korean hymns, and stood up and sat down in the order the church service bulletin dictated. I constantly fought drowsiness and boredom as I entertained myself with my imagination. With no solid youth group or community to grow in, I simply went through the motions week after week, year after year. Church was basically a chore.

My parents tried to the best of their ability to

faithfully increase the church member count and be Christ-like to them, so I held onto the hope that a youth group would eventually emerge. I carried a child-like eagerness to fellowship with other kids my age and learn about the Bible. There were hopeful moments where there would either be enough kids or a potential youth pastor in our midst. It seemed like we were on the verge of breakthrough, but for whatever reason it would fall through and that hope would dissipate. I felt frustrated because after all the years of sacrificing, giving, and being obedient to this system called church, I got nothing in return.

At the start of high school, my parents let my brother and I attend and fellowship at a middle-sized church where we finally got to experience what youth group was about: retreats, Bible studies, basically the whole package. It was great, but by then my heart towards God was filled with bitterness, hatred, and fear. I was done living the lifestyle of faith. This led me to seeking after God or the truth in seemingly more concrete things like science, logic, reasoning, and wisdom. I believed that if I knew enough about God, I would grasp Him. It was important for me to understand how this world worked so I could come to terms with my circumstances. This brought me temporary satisfaction and comfort.

College rolled around, and I was sold. I loved UC Santa Barbara and all of the newfound freedom that I had suddenly obtained. I thought I was free at last. At this point, I was sick of being told what to do and of blindly believing in God for the sake of religion. I checked out a few Christian organizations, but I quickly dropped those because I was more excited to explore Isla Vista and what it had to offer. My wounded heart coupled with the deep desire to know and experience something greater than myself manifested in my curiosity in the party scene and substances.

During spring quarter of my freshman year, I heard about Isla Vista Church from Andy Do and a few others from EPIC, an Asian American campus ministry that I attended. I eventually wanted a home church, so I mustered up enough courage to give it a try. I walked in, sat down on a pew, and immediately felt uncomfortable because I was only familiar with the structure of a conservative church service. I hadn't known this beforehand, but Isla Vista Church values hearing the voice of God and uses the spiritual gifts to build up the Body. The concept of spiritual gifts, the voice of God, or anything remotely within the supernatural realm was foreign to me. I felt particularly sinful because of my lifestyle, so I fervently asked God to forgive me for my sins.

As soon as I finished that prayer, the unexpected happened: the two ladies that led worship, Braelyn Montgomery and Michelle Quezada, saw that the worship was winding down, so one of them exclaimed, "You guys, let's get up out of our seats and rejoice in the Lord through dancing!"

Soon enough, I was the only one seated as everyone was up dancing and rejoicing in the Lord! I distinctly remember freaking out at the prophetic dance occurring in the aisles. I again scanned the crowd for Andy Do, only to find him dancing as well! I bolted out of the church service and biked straight to my dorm nearly in tears. This experience was such a culture shock. I felt scared, but I knew deep down these people had something that I was missing. I had to go back and see this curiosity through.

I attended Isla Vista Church on the first Sunday of the fall quarter of my second year. I specifically prayed for God not to call me up to the front because of my fear of man. Oddly enough, Jason asked the new members of the church to come up to the front to be blessed and prayed for since it was the beginning of the school year. I told God, "I'm sorry, Father. I'm going to have to let you down on this one. You know I have the fear of man."

Oddly enough again, Jason spoke out right after that thought with something along the lines of, "I feel like there are some of you out there that need to fight the fear of man."

I had begun to suspect this wasn't just coincidence, but God using the situation to say something to me. I mustered up the courage and went up in front of the entire congregation with a few others. A few people laid hands on me and started praying and prophesying. This prayer session was my first introduction to the prophetic, and I cannot stress how significant this moment was for me. I can't recall his name, but a man with a round stature and white hair told me that God wanted me to know that those who are prophetic—especially that those who worship God through dance—have full control over their movements. He then mentioned 1 Corinthians 14, which speaks on intelligibility in worship. This struck me hard because prior to that moment, the supernatural frightened me. I heard that those under the prophetic state would temporarily lose control of their movement and conscience. I was so struck with love because the prophetic word was specifically catered towards me, which meant that God cared about me. Shortly after that service, I wholeheartedly committed my life to Christ!

I was in awe of how well the Isla Vista Church family stewarded the culture of hearing God's voice and valued doing life together as a family. They had so much freedom because they knew their identities as sons and daughters of God. I have never wanted to be a part of any community as much as this, and that is saying a lot considering my history with ministries.

This proved true with Jesus Burgers as well. My first Jesus Burgers night was during Halloween, which was a big deal because Halloween is one of the biggest partying events of the school year. I loved how raw and open the ministry was in loving and caring for the partygoers of Isla Vista. We weren't shoving religion on them, but showing them the genuine love of Christ. Evangelism was actually fun for the first time. What drew my attention more than anything was the prophetic ministry happening across the street. A few Jesus Burgers people stood behind a large wooden sign that read: "Free spiritual readings." I walked over to see what it was all about, and what I saw completely blew my mind. Scott, the head honcho of that ministry, and a few others were prophetically speaking truth and life into people coming up. They were also praying for supernatural healing! I saw so many people get touched by what God had to say to them and also saw many people get healed and delivered of injuries and sicknesses. No matter what circumstances I was going through in life, I knew that when I was doing ministry in the streets, I was in the right place. I stuck around the sign week after week to observe, learn, and receive what they carried. Eventually, I joined the prophetic sign ministry.

I didn't know this at the time, but the prophetic sign ministry greatly appealed to me because I desperately craved for proof of God all throughout my life. Gradually, through spending time at the sign and doing life with the IVC family, I learned to hear God's voice by connecting with Him in the secret place.

There would be so many instances where people would exclaim, "Woah, how did you know that about me?!" after having a prophetic word spoken over them, or say, "No way . . . the pain is completely gone!" after we prayed for healing.

I felt so much joy when people were tangibly touched by God, and I considered it a victory when they left the sign feeling blessed after prayer or good conversation.

Out of all of the testimonies, the one that stands out the most actually happened in the front yard of the Jesus Burgers house around three o'clock in the morning after a successful night. The sign was taken in and a handful of us were relaxing, when a man from around the corner asked for a cigarette. When he realized we didn't have any to offer, he quickly changed the topic to his negative relationship with his dad. We told him to come on over, and he stumbled in.

If I recall correctly, his name was Blu. He told us about how he had had to grow up fast because he had to fend off his abusive dad while basically becoming the man of the family and taking care of his mom and his siblings. He also revealed to us that he had slight nerve damage on the lower half of his body, so he couldn't bend down all the way. He had had a hard life; it was written all over his face. I could tell he was defensive and ready to get physical at any sign of judgment or aggression from any of us. It was a very tense moment!

One of us boldly went up to him and proclaimed that God would completely heal him of his nerve damage. It was an Elijah-and-the-prophets-of-Baal moment. God just had to show up! By the grace of God, he allowed us to lay hands on him and pray for him. He then took a step, with a doubtful face, to test it out.

He tested his left leg out and softly muttered, "What . . . ?"

Excitement began to stir up in the atmosphere.

He tested out his right leg, then looked up at us with big eyes. He proceeded to bend all the way down to touch his toes without any pain.

After much processing, he muttered as he looked up into the sky, "I haven't been able to do that in years. Thank you, God."

A few of us asked God for a prophetic word and released it to him, and that caught his attention.

He said curiously, "God told you that?"

One of us responded, "Yeah, we speak to God and He speaks to us."

At this point, he was awestruck. We exchanged numbers before he left, but I'm sure that night stuck out to him. It was a privilege of mine to be able to witness Blu tangibly experience God that night. That night was just another testament of how God loves and cares about us, even in the small things.

I had a revelation one time that God was with me in every crushing and seemingly hopeless moment in my life. I cherished this truth in the innermost place of my heart because I believed for most of my life that God was this distant and unreachable entity. But the truth was that He had been with me all along! I had not realized what the victory of the cross and the tearing of the veil meant. The truth is that we have full access with nothing separating us from God! His plan all along was to bring the lost into His family, and it is a privilege to share what I have received.

NOTHING
BUT THE
TRUTH

YVETTE JOHNSON

I once lived a life narrated by a self-imposed reality. I recognized my own efforts as the prevalent wind blowing my life into motion. Only I defined who I was. Before knowing God, life seemed uncomplicated: listen to your heart, learn what your passionate about, and do everything in your power to fulfill your dreams.

Though my simple life philosophy got me through my days with a smile, it wasn't enough to explain humanity's shortcomings or even my own. As I leaned fully on my understanding that only humans and randomness controlled the situations in the world, I couldn't make sense out of humanity's failures. Eventually, my suffering exposed to me how complicated I really was. My physical limitations as a finite being led me to fail, and I lacked the ability to pick up the shattered pieces of my heart by my willpower alone.

My interest in discovering true inner peace ignited a pursuit of living a life of absolute Truth. In seeking Truth, circumstances led me to open my heart up to a God who loves. This God possesses the

only strength powerful enough to pick up the broken pieces of my heart and lead me through a healing
process back into the person He intended me to be.
No matter how much I accomplished I could never be
fully content with myself because I didn't fully know
myself. Once I said yes to knowing God, He showed
me who I was by showing me who He is. I learned
that I didn't need to lean on anything in this world
because He created me to stand strong, deeply rooted
in His unfailing love.

I come from a very loving and strong family in a
beautiful small town just above the American River
in Northern California. During my early years, I spent
many nights sitting outside with my dad stargazing.
The quiet air of my childhood whispered encouragement to dream big. Before I knew it, dance found me.
This extreme passion shifted my gaze from the stars
to my dance technique. I remember not even thinking
twice about being tired as my mom drove me straight
from school to dance everyday. In school, my peers
didn't really know me without dance, and frankly I
didn't know myself without it either. My teachers encouraged me to pursue this discipline since not only
did I love it, but I was not too bad at it either.

Dance taught me wonderful skills that still rest
in me today, including discipline, patience, focus, and
perseverance. I saw the type of person I wanted to be
and learned how to control, sometimes even manipulate, circumstances around me to cater to my creation
of my ideal version of me. This resulted in a very high
GPA, recognition as a talented dancer, and, unfortunately, a well-concealed eating disorder. Facing the
reality of my problems didn't usher me closer to my
goals, so I learned how to swallow negative feelings
and wear a smile whatever the circumstance. I figured
that my insecurities would go away someday if I kept

pushing towards the things that made me feel worthy.

Fortunately, the warm love from my family led me to feel guilty about doing things I needed to lie about. My heart sprung a leak. After confessing my eating disorder to my mom when I was sixteen, to my surprise, she hugged me and said we would get through this together. She showed me love in my shortcomings and shame when I expected disappointment. That was my first understanding of the Father's heart: He loves me wherever I'm at. From that point on, honesty became one of my biggest values, even when it is difficult.

After graduating from high school, I decided that the wisest thing for me to do was to get a degree in dance. Choosing to go to school at UCSB was very unlike me at that point, as it was my dream to leave California for New York. Though I didn't know it was God, His wisdom spoke to my seventeen-year-old, non-believing self in the form of a gut feeling, "There is something good for you in Santa Barbara." Praise God I listened.

The summer after high school, I began practicing yoga and fell in love. For the first time, I was inspired to inquire about life's meaning. Not only was I questioning everything I had ever believed in, including God, but also I felt convicted of living a life absent of integrity. If God was real, I couldn't just halfway acknowledge Him, I needed to be all in or all out. After retreating to South Lake Tahoe with a bunch of my new yogi friends, I got the opportunity to listen to the teachings of a local Buddhist monk. When I arrived back home, my eighteen-year-old, pre-college self denounced the existence of God. I felt so clever and free to have figured this all out on my own. I saw the fear in my mom and aunt's faces. While they may not have been walking in full relationship with God at the time, they feared Him and knew He was real.

My first year as a dance major at UCSB was amazing. I learned that life's riches existed inside and outside of the dance studio. I made strong friendships, studied all of the major modern philosophers, spent a lot of time reading in coffee shops, and got parts in every dance show I auditioned for. Still having my greatest priority being my dance career, I was protected from ever partying too hard. I'd go out to Isla Vista, but I thought I had it all figured out. I'd drink enough to loosen up, stay out, and dance innocently at parties with friends, but always be back home early enough to feel great the next day to dance. I made an effort to get to know everyone in the department; in doing so, I realized that some of the cool and loving people in the department loved Jesus. This confused me, for up until then all the Christians I knew were boring, hypocritical, and usually weren't good dancers because they prioritized God-oriented things instead of dance. However, I decided that for these Christians their faith was sweet and part of who they were, so I developed friendships with some of them.

Life was going in a direction that always led me to happiness until an unwanted circumstance interfered. Sophomore year, right before a big dance show that I got a leading role in, I noticed an incredible pain in my left front ribcage. I was desperate, and one of the Jesus loving dancers, Meredith, could tell.

I could see the compassion in her eyes, and she took a bold step towards a very advertised agnostic and asked, "Can I pray for your rib?"

Confused, slightly apprehensive, and incredibly desperate, I said, "Please!"

After she prayed, I biked home that night staring at the stars and had a funny little dialogue with God that started like, "Hi, God, sorry it's been a while. If

You are real, can You do something miraculous?" He healed my fractured rib that night. I woke up the next day and performed. I was stoked, amazed, and scared out of my mind.

Despite a miracle, I still wasn't fully convinced of God's existence. Nevertheless, the quotes located on the Yogi tea bags I drank from seemed to be speaking important messages. A particular quote kept creeping into my mornings, "You must live for something bigger and greater than yourself."

Whoops. I realized I wasn't exactly doing that. Up until that point I never really knew how to live for anything other than myself. I couldn't help but continually ponder the meaning of my existence.

The following Christmas break at my parent's home included a lot of inquiry beside the American River after my yoga practice. If God was real, He needed to show Himself to me again, because when using my own logic, there was no way I could understand this God who heals.

One day at the end of yoga class during *Savasana*, Sanskrit for "corpse pose," the teacher simply stated, "Doubt the doubt." She followed with the command, "Acknowledge the infinite presence of God."

Though seemingly fluffy for me, I stopped my thoughts and waited. In an instance, I felt the Presence of God. I can't explain to you what exactly it was, but I felt whole, connected, and alive. From that point on, I knew 100 percent that God was real.

After my God realization, I came back to school, and Meredith and I were cast together in a dance piece choreographed by Lindsay, another one of these Jesus dancers that I didn't understand but really liked. Her piece portrayed the testimony of her friend encountering and conquering battles with several demons in his life, including fear, lust, and envy.

During rehearsals, we would talk about this battle of light versus darkness, and it all made so much sense. Light always conquered the dark, and God was good! Everything that we concluded seemed to be previously known in my heart, as if it was all coming back to me. It was interesting to me that we could all speak so logically, yet artistically, about something that seemed so feathery and silly to me before. I'd walk by the infamous Jesus Burgers house on DP Friday nights and feel important to know Lindsay, who lived at the house. Once I sat with her by the fire pit with her Jesus friends. I felt like I was part of something greater than myself. It was simple: these people just confidently loved, as if they knew something fuller than I did. I was too afraid to ask about how they loved so well and figured that God would speak to me about it in due time.

After continually denying Meredith's invitations to church, it finally felt right to attend on Easter Sunday. We went to Reality Santa Barbara, and Britt Merrick preached the gospel of Jesus Christ. As he told us about the story of Jesus, there was no doubt in my mind that kept me from hearing, so it was only logically inevitable that I would stand up and say yes to following this Jesus. In the moment that I heard this account of the salvation of humanity it all made sense. I felt at peace. Jesus set me free from the bondage that kept me away from receiving God's Love! That was the beginning of the rest of my life. Since then, I've been through the highest of highs and the lowest of lows, but all of these moments have been secure and rich because God has been there with me.

My life before knowing God was built around a whole lot of ignorance. Facing my shortcomings, fears, and failures once scared me, because I found that I was not strong enough to clean up the leftover baggage of past regret. Looking back, this was an accurate notion, for without God's grace, humans can only deal with a limited amount of junk. God has slowly revealed the reality of my heart to me, and without the greater reality of Jesus reigning true in my walk today, there is no way I would be able to step forward without fear.

During my senior year at UCSB, I lived at the Jesus Burgers house and greeted fellow dancers at the BBQ like Lindsay had done before. They would all come so excited to know someone who lived at the infamous JB house. My senior project explored the idea of walking into the purity of Heaven by facing fears. I invited my cast of five dancers to be open about sharing their fears, bringing them to the light, and walking through them, an honor that I will never forget. Spiritual dialogue was a regular part of rehearsal, and God led the way of a very rich creative process. I guess one could say I came full circle.

But it wasn't just living at the house or succeeding in the choreographic realm that created my identity. Once I acknowledged what God was saying, my entire perspective of the world and my life shifted. It became so easy to love my friends, dance in love instead of fear, and truly love the creation that God made me to be. It was like God gave me His heart for them by showing me His heart for me. Even now my eyes well up as I think about how precious those individuals are. I recognize that something in me shifted. I wouldn't say that life got easier, but it got real. Truth truly set me free. I can face the reality of the darkness because the reality of the Light is stronger.

PUTTING
GOD FIRST

MIKE SELF

My story starts with stripper poles, a vast amount of partying, and a long time of satisfying my own sinful nature. Unfortunately, the constant indulgence of the world's pleasures captured my passions until my college years, when God introduced me to Jason Lomelino and Isla Vista Church through Jesus Burgers. There was always a hidden desire in me to put God first, but it was a constant struggle. Through Jesus Burgers, the course of my life was drastically changed, and I began the journey of becoming the man of God I am today. I now know He had one desire for me my entire life: to put Him first in everything I do.

Growing up in Orange County, California, I always found some way to get myself into trouble. I liked to test my limits and see how far my boundaries would go. Unfortunately, I learned lessons the hard way. My family was Christ centered, and I went to church and believed in God, but the truth of it all never really made sense or clicked with me. In high school, I was a rebel and hung out with the wrong groups. I got myself into a lot of trouble. I barely graduated high school, with a 46 percent absentee rate and the lowest eligible GPA allowed to get a diploma and walk at the graduation ceremony.

Even though it appeared I was a major mess, I was always a very good salesman and naturally excelled at business. I had a good job ending my high school career, but I was still uncertain what I wanted to do with my life. I was faced with the major decision every young adult must go through: Do I go to college? Obviously I hated school as my track record spoke for itself. In the midst of this life decision, I got myself into a major incident, which God used to change me for good.

One night, while still living in Orange County, I went to a party in my brand new Acura TL. I ended up getting behind the wheel drunk that night and completely totaled my brand new car. Thankfully, God protected me from any serious injury, but I did get a DUI. Even though I may not have realized it, God had gotten my attention: I needed to get my life together and go to college.

Santa Barbara City College was the best option for me, as there was no way any university was going to accept me. I left my good job, all my friends, a totaled car, and made the move to Santa Barbara. I enrolled at City College and landed in Isla Vista looking for a fresh start. My parents had been very supportive during this time and strongly advised me to make some serious lifestyle changes. But it didn't stick.

Little did I know, I was actually moving to one of the biggest party schools in the country. With the best college parties at my fingertips, my ability to meet new people, and a strong desire to have fun, I was straight back to my old ways in no time. The path of destruction was upon me, and if something major didn't happen quickly, I was doomed for darkness.

However, God had a plan, and He was avid about getting my attention.

One night as I cruised Del Playa with a group of my friends, I got separated from them and somehow stumbled into Jesus Burgers. I always knew there were some Jesus people who lived on this street and gave out free burgers, but I never got a chance to check it out, until that night. As I stumbled up to get my hamburger, a friendly guy introduced himself to me. His name was Jason.

As we began to talk, I felt that Jason was the ear that I needed that night. I was able to tell him what I was going through, and that I knew I was on the wrong path. I even remember telling him, "If something doesn't change soon, I am going to die in my sinful nature." I didn't know this then, but God had already revealed this to him in the Spirit as I was standing in line.

Jason accepted me with open arms and offered to be my friend. Jason showed me that God wanted me back, and he made it clear to me that I was tired of the life I was living. This was a ground-breaking conversation for me. All of a sudden, I felt light coming into my dark situation. Something clicked: Life is really about Jesus and putting God first. This man was speaking the truth that led me right to Jesus. As we talked, I knew this was the change I was looking for. We exchanged contact information, and Jason offered to meet up with me the following week. This is exactly what I needed. In retrospect, that night at Jesus Burgers truly changed the course of my life.

Jason and I started meeting up weekly. Over the course of time, my life started to gain a Biblical foundation. I remember the first time Jason came over to my house to read the Bible together. He was so kind, despite seeing that I had a stripper pole in my living room. There was no judgment with him, just love, and that was exactly what my heart needed. I needed to know that God loved and accepted me and that I was fully capable of keeping Him first. We decided to meet in a park from then on, but I'm happy to say that I did get rid of that stripper pole.

As our relationship grew, Jason taught me about the truth and the awesomeness of God. My heart began to open as I formed friendships within the Isla Vista Church community. For once in my life, I knew that I was on the path of putting God first, and sure enough my life started to change and gain stability. I could feel myself building a foundation that would last me forever.

This was the foundation I needed to settle on. Don't get me wrong, my change of ways and walking in the Spirit did not happen overnight. It was a process, and I still believe it is a process. However, I needed the foundation of faith in Jesus to walk through the fires of life. As my spiritual formation progressed, I firmly came to believe that Jesus died on the cross for my sins, loves me, and is there for me anytime I need Him.

I vividly remember one conversation with Jason in which I had an epiphany that following God was not about religion, rather it was about a relationship. That was the key thing that got me. It was the fact that God was my friend and that I could have a personal relationship with Him. I learned that it wasn't necessarily about going to church every Sunday and that if you didn't you weren't going to hell. It's about repenting, having faith, and maintaining a solid relationship with God while creating your foundation on a solid rock—the solid Rock of God and all His glory! To seal the deal, Jason eventually baptized me on a beach in Isla Vista. My life had taken a drastic turn, and God was becoming the first priority.

Due to the foundation of truth I was able to find through Jesus Burgers, I ended up graduating from community college with a 4.0 on President's Honor Roll. This prepared me to get accepted to my dream university, USC Marshall School of Business. No one ever thought I would be able to do this as I failed nearly my entire high school career, but by the grace of God I was able to make these huge accomplishments. Jason helped me realize that I can do all things through Christ. He taught me how to drop the things that were hindering me and to receive the Holy Spirit. These simple truths set me up to experience amazing breakthroughs, and they continue to be the foundation of my success. I owe my life to Jesus. Through the ministry of Jesus Burgers, God gave me exactly what I needed: a fresh revelation of who He is, who I am, and a community of believers to walk with me through life. I am now fully capable of putting and keeping Him first in my life.

Since leaving Isla Vista and attending USC, God has empowered me to start my dream company that He continues to pour His favor on. My career is on the rise, but most importantly I am growing in God and keeping Him first. No matter what struggles come my way, I know that Jesus made me to be a conqueror and that with God all things are possible. As God continues to grow me, I continue to dream of how my life will be used to bring the Kingdom of God to earth. My heart is to spread the love of God through empowering people and ministries. God has gifted me with business, and I plan to use these skills for His glory.

I will forever be extremely grateful that God used Jesus Burgers and my time with Jason and the Isla Vista Community to direct the course of my life. It's amazing what God can do through a simple hamburger and a group of people who chose to show me the love of God. My experience through Jesus Burgers has been the best thing that has ever happened to me.

2

HOPE

Now may the God of hope fill you with all joy and
peace in believing, so that you will abound in hope
by the power of the Holy Spirit.

Romans 15:13 (NASB)

ANCHORED

HOPE CURRAN

ebrews 6:19 says, "Hope is an anchor of the soul, strong and secure, where Jesus enters in on our behalf." My parents gave me the name Hope, and from that day twenty years ago until now, I have come to realize the depth and wondrous meaning it holds. The dictionary says that hope desires, aspires, dreams, plans, and expects without fear of the future. Living in Isla Vista, I yearn for my hope to be anchored in Jesus and that my life will reflect that.

I grew up the youngest of four children in a caring, Christian home of loving missionary parents. I knew all the right answers in Sunday school and had a lot of head knowledge of the Bible. However, by high school I craved more than just the intellectual aspects of Christianity.

I first learned about the gifts of the Holy Spirit going into my sophomore year while attending a life-changing camp designed for missionary kids. That summer God gave me the desire to make my faith my own, filled me with His Spirit, and started to build my heart for sharing the gospel of Jesus with those around me. I decided to take my extracurricular

activities to the next level and start a club at my public high school. Perhaps a foreshadowing of my future
with Jesus Burgers, I called it "Lunch with Jesus." I
became the "Jesus freak" and "Godly girl" in school
and realized that following Jesus requires radical
faith and a secure identity in Christ. Senior year
AP classes, early morning swim practices, jazz band,
French night classes, and art portfolios were not only
my final attempt to try to push my way into the best
college possible but also how God prepared the way
for me to come to UCSB. He led me to study art and
global studies, to swim, and eventually, to live in the
Jesus Burgers house.

I took a recruiting trip to UCSB for their swim-
ming and diving team. Coach Gregg Wilson happened to be a strong believer, and he had two girls
who also loved Jesus host me. My preconceived no-
tions of UCSB being a party school and not knowing
how I would fit in were confirmed as I sat awkwardly
at a party on a couch with a red cup filled with water,
not knowing what to do with my hands. The amazing part about this recruiting trip was that I saw both
ends of the spectrum: the reality of the party scene as
well as the encouraging testimonies of how God was
redeeming Isla Vista from my hosts.

"Hope, the swim team and this city need light.
You need to come here." After the campus tour,
Coach Gregg pulled me aside and told me that after
forty years of coaching at UCSB there were very few
Christians who maintained their faith all four years.
He explained the difficulty of staying anchored in
your faith in a party town and on the swim team. He
looked at me in the eyes and said, "Remember, light
shines brightest in the darkness." These words rang
in my ears as I left Isla Vista that weekend, happy to
have made it out alive.

Decisions needed to be made as college deadlines approached. Coach Gregg called me in late April and told me I had two days to make my decision, otherwise my guaranteed acceptance and spot on the team would be given to someone else. I had no idea where I wanted to spend the next four years of my life, but I trusted that God knew. I went straight to the Bible in this time of panic and found myself in the first chapter of Luke,

"You my child, will be called a child of the most high . . . You will go on before the lord to shine on those living in darkness, and in the shadow of death, to guide our feet in the path of peace" (Luke 1:76–79).

The moment I read the word "darkness" it was as if the Holy Spirit was screaming, "Isla Vista." I knew immediately that God wanted to pop my safe and comfortable Christian bubble and take me on a glorious and life-changing adventure. So, I said yes. God affirms this decision still to this day as I see His plan unfold in Isla Vista, a town of hope and redemption.

Flash forward to new student orientation. Rather than attending the overwhelming amount of parent meetings like a normal dad, my campus-minister father went for a prayer walk in Isla Vista and stumbled upon the Jesus Burgers table where they were selling *Jesus Burgers: Volume 1.* He picked up a few copies of the book and obtained phone numbers of people involved with the ministry I would later consider my family. One Friday night in the middle of fall quarter, I spontaneously went to Upper Room before a big swim team party. As we worshiped and danced to God, I had this overwhelming feeling that I had come home. It seemed I had finally found my people. The creativity, love, peace, and sheer joy of serving God spilled from the Upper Room and overflowed onto Del Playa. This community became a family instantly.

My sophomore year I lived in a cute little purple house on Sueño Road, which means "dream" in Spanish. That year God met me through dreams and continued to give me vision and opportunity to shine His light through darkness. Swim team, Bible studies, and witnessing a teammate accept Christ were just a few of the promises God fulfilled that year. When friends started signing leases for junior year, I wasn't sure whom to house with, but I kept hearing God say, "WAIT." Waiting also meant trusting Him with the outcome. Jason mentioned openings at the Jesus Burgers house and encouraged me to pray and think about moving in for the next year. In January, I said yes to living in the ministry house, months after my friends had signed their lease without me.

Isaiah 61 became the theme verse of 2014—proclaiming the year of the Lord's favor to Isla Vista by living in a house that kindles community, love, and light. Later in the spring, this verse surfaced again after the Isla Vista shootings. God's promise of trading the ashes of a party city for a crown of beauty and to bring joy amidst mourning put Jesus Burgers in a perfect position to minister to the people of Isla Vista.

Throughout the spring, our little college town experienced an overwhelming amount of death and destruction. This made me realize that our physical lives can end at any time, but life isn't about us. You are not meant to live everyday as if it's your last; rather, you are meant to live each day as if it's the last for those around you. Jesus demonstrated ultimate servanthood by giving His life and dying on a cross, rising from the dead, and bringing humanity into the fullness of life. every Friday night, Jesus Burgers is an outlet for people to be just like Jesus. I know if

Jesus were to come to Isla Vista, He would be right there in the thick of it on Del Playa, giving out burgers and starting relationships with those who crave them most. Go where Jesus would go. Love those He would love.

My favorite job on Fridays is as a greeter for people in line to get burgers. I feel like a mix between a traffic officer asking people to please not cut and a waitress asking people what they're really hungry for in life. I get to meet hundreds of new friends each week and hear their incredible stories as well as share mine. Strangers are not so strange once you get talking.

One Jesus Burgers that was especially overflowing with the sparkle of the Holy Spirit was the night Jenn Bowman told me she would be living in the Jesus Burgers house with me. Tears formed in my eyes, not caused by emotion, but rather by the smoke of the grill blinding us as we designed the most intricate ketchup hearts and mustard crosses on buns that would be devoured in a matter of seconds by hungry partygoers that ate their long awaited prize.

The burgers eventually ran out, and the warmth of the fire looked inviting to our cold hands on this winter night. A group of girls, hungry and freezing, waited by the grill even though the burgers had run out. I apologized and offered them a free blessing that might fill their soul's appetite. We held hands and stood in a circle, and another group of girls standing nearby joined in as well. As I prayed for each girl individually and blessed their friendships and studies, more girls came and joined the circle, hungry for truth and love to be poured into their hearts. Tears fell from the makeup-covered eyes of a girl celebrating her birthday; she had never had someone pray for her. It was late and the yard was clearing out. I told them all about the life of Jesus and the love He offers.

There are thousands of people to love on, but my first ministry is to my swim team, all of whom live in Isla Vista. God has showed me time and time again that my identity does not lie in the points I score at swim meets or how fast I swim, but that He has me specifically in Isla Vista to be a light on my swim team and to love them. Love does not judge, love *does*. Some Friday nights I take my ministry outside of 6686 Del Playa and will meet up with teammates and friends to go to parties. I choose not to drink and am available for anyone who is having a rough night. I have started this habit of drawing an anchor on my left wrist before going out in Isla Vista, whether for Jesus Burgers or a party with teammates. This tattoo wanna-be has allowed me to share about how my parents gave me the name Hope and how Jesus has become the anchor of my soul, especially amidst the waves of Isla Vista. Wearing my anchor, drinking my water, and dancing like a fool by myself, I think I've found my place in the party scene: to be in it and not of it as I share the hope Jesus offers.

HE RESCUED ME

JENN BOWMAN

I woke up with my head spinning, trying to piece together the night before. The room still reeked of alcohol as I slowly dragged myself out of bed to make it to the bathroom. My reflection in the mirror was unrecognizable. As I stared at the makeup smeared all over my sunken-in face, the images of the previous night came back to me. The blaring music, the hands of a boy whom I didn't even know, and the "friends" I began the night with who were now nowhere to be found. How did I even get here? Why was I still wearing my outfit from the night before? Then, before I could even begin to answer these questions, I was crouched down on the tile floor too nauseated to focus on anything but feeling sick. This was just my typical Saturday morning as a sophomore in college. And even though the morning was typical, I could never get used to the growing feeling of emptiness.

Looking back, this was what I did to cope. This was who I thought I was. I used the parties, drugs, alcohol, and boys to drown out and numb the repressed pain and emptiness I was carrying within me. But more significantly, it was what I did to ignore the harsh reality of being a twenty-year-old girl with ab-solutely no sense of self-worth. I was someone trying to fill a void. If you had told me during that time that Jesus was the answer, I wouldn't have believed you. I honestly felt that I was too far gone to be rescued.

But deep down, I really knew I wanted to be res-cued. I've wanted to be rescued for as long as I can re-member. I just knew it would have to take something bigger than myself. As a child, I saw divorce destroy my family. What led up to the divorce and what re-sulted from the divorce left me with a deep emptiness that weighed on me throughout my life. As many chil-dren often do, I blamed myself for the abusive calam-ity and sadness that possessed my home.

As I grew older, this pain and sadness quickly morphed into full rebellion and a shattered self-esteem. I often questioned if God even existed as I sought purpose and meaning for my life. Ultimately, I didn't see the point of life. Why would God allow people to experience this much sadness, pain, and emptiness? The most defeating reality I accepted was that if God did exist, He obviously didn't care all that much about me.

It was during this time that my relationship with my father became estranged for multiple years. I cut myself off from so many people and let bulimia become my closest friend. By the end of my fresh-man year of high school, my life became a great con-cern to my grandparents on both sides of my family. They agreed that the best decision was to arrange to have me live in Northern California with my mater-nal grandmother. And even though my grandparents poured so much love onto me, my heart was still so resistant to accept it.

Instead, I sought fulfillment in drinking, experi-menting with drugs, and sex. My self-worth was reliant on worldly impulses and finding the next "high." This was mostly found in boys, but often it included shoplifting, partying, sneaking out late at night, and putting myself in extremely dangerous situations for the sake of feeling "alive." Like my friends in similar circumstances, things quickly spiraled out of control. After a year of run-ins with the police, almost failing most of my classes, and noticeably watching my body wither away, I began not only to admit I needed help but also to seek it.

God began working within me, though I was unaware of it at the time. Through the struggle, I began to look at my life differently and take the necessary steps in order to change. I started to break away from unhealthy friendships and was put into intensive treatment for my bulimia, which consisted of seeing two psychologists, a psychiatrist, a nutritionist, and a cardiologist on a regular basis to monitor my disorder.

In a way, this was the first time that I noticeably felt God trying to save me from the destruction I was headed towards. Near the end of recovery, a friend invited me to go on a mission trip with her to Mexico for spring break. During this mission trip, I experienced my first glimpse into God's love and the unfamiliar territory of people living their lives for Christ. Even though I never fully accepted God into my heart, I clung to my friends from that trip until the end of high school. And while I considered myself a Christian at the time, I was still sleeping with my then boyfriend, drinking heavily, and struggling with bulimia behind closed doors. My family was so proud of me for turning my life around so drastically, but I knew deep down that my heart had stayed the same.

Unfortunately, after moving to Isla Vista for my freshman year, things quickly spiraled down once again. Go figure. If I had been willing to let my guard down and fully let Jesus into my heart during high school, maybe college would have been pleasantly different. But I continued my old habits of searching for my self-worth in alcohol, drugs, boys, and my crippling reliance on bulimia to cope with the emptiness. This vicious cycle lasted for two years, until the end of my sophomore year.

At this point, I cracked. I went home to my grandmother's for the summer, and I hit my rock bottom. I immediately fell into the deepest depression I had ever experienced. Everyday, I heard the incessant voice of the enemy trying to persuade me to give up my life. I completely stopped eating, rarely left the house, and slept all day. My spare time consisted of staring at walls, bawling my eyes out, and praying to God for him to take my life so that I wouldn't have to go through with doing it myself.

I almost dropped out of school that summer, but I mustered up some willpower to stay enrolled and continue living in Isla Vista. I really wasn't expecting anything to change or for things to get better at all. I just knew that living in Isla Vista would be easier on my family since I felt like a burden. I knew my grandmother was living in constant fear of what I would do if left by myself. And I knew what I ultimately wanted to do. I felt trapped in depression, and the only door I could see leading out of it was death.

My Christian friends from high school knew of my circumstances and connected me to a girl named Hope who lived in Isla Vista. The day we met was also the first day she brought me to Isla Vista Church. Shortly after, I found myself chatting with the pastor, Jason, and he told me that I was not defined by my current circumstances, but instead defined by the love of Jesus Christ. Over time, a lot of the things people were saying about Jesus got me thinking, and

I felt my heart begin to soften.

When I first came to this church, I was so awe-struck by how nice and loving everyone was to me. I couldn't understand it, and I naturally kept trying to find a loophole. As I stuck around and began to connect with others from Isla Vista Church, I was introduced to the Jesus Burgers ministry. When I showed up to Jesus Burgers for the first time, I realized that I was not the only one they were being loving towards. They were being kind and serving food to everyone, believers and nonbelievers alike.

These experiences got me thinking a lot about God because I saw something different in the people who had a real relationship with Him. One person in particular I noticed this difference in was a girl named Ava. She was the first person to help me discover the power of having a personal relationship with Jesus. Little did I know, Ava had been keeping an eye on me and had been carrying God's heart for my life. It was completely clear to her how broken I was. She could discern that I was still dealing with bulimia, anxiety, depression, and insecurity. We barely knew each other, but right off the bat God called her to dedicate multiple hours a week to help me out of my season of darkness.

Ava was a friend who constantly reminded me of my new identity in Christ and that the illness and pain I was dealing with was not God's will for my life. God used her to encourage, comfort, and teach me about His character. Over the months we spent together, God steadily began to soften my heart, acknowledge my brokenness, and earn my trust. As I grew deeper in relationship with God, I understood that He forgave me for everything, including my lingering past. It was His love that gave me the strength to forgive my family and to start anew. By God's grace,

I began to feel my life being restored. Jesus was truly rescuing me and surrounding me by supportive people to help me through the process.

Believe it or not, I now live at the Jesus Burgers house in Isla Vista, serving the community with love and purpose. I still can't believe how far I've come from the person I once was, but I can confidently say that it was Jesus who rescued me and gave me a hope and a future. I am radically blessed to have found such amazing people who live their lives for Christ in every way. We are continually growing as a family and learning to show unconditional love and acceptance to our community in Isla Vista. Our main focus is to spread the love of God to anyone and everyone that is willing to receive it.

At Jesus Burgers, when I look out at the streets filled with girls my age rushing to parties, I see my old self in them. I see the insecurity, the hopelessness, the addictions, the pain, the lack of self-worth, and the thirst for something greater, something that only the love of their Father can satisfy. God relentlessly pursues them to rescue them from the pain, like He did for me. I desire for girls to relate to my experiences in hopes of giving them an answer. I want to inspire girls my age to find their identity in the most beautiful and loving man who has ever existed—a man named Jesus, who looks at them with love, value, and acceptance. I know that I am a living testimony of the redemption found in an authentic relationship with Jesus Christ. He has given me life, and that is why I am so passionate about giving it to others.

"But because of His great love for us, God, who is rich in mercy, made us alive with Christ even when we were dead in transgressions—it is by grace you have been saved" (Ephesians 2: 4–5).

FOUND
AMONGST
THE LOST

ELIJAH SIMMONS

As I retrace my steps back to where my walk with Jesus began, it's hard to believe that I almost threw away everything I've been blessed with in pursuit of a life that wasn't meant for me. I was born into a Christian family with parents who love each other, and we went to church together every Sunday. One night when I was about ten-years-old, I laid awake in my bed wondering if I would go to Heaven when I died. Had I been too mean to my little brother or talked back to my mom too many times to deserve being saved? Remembering what I had learned in church, I thanked God for sending His son to die for my sins and accepted Jesus as my savior. At the time, I had no idea what it meant to have a personal relationship with Jesus. For the next several years, I continued going to church with my family and saying my prayers at night, but I always felt like something was missing.

As I got older and my friends started smoking and drinking, I knew that joining them would disappoint God, but in the moment I was more concerned with being accepted. At first it all seemed pretty harmless.

In an effort to justify my actions, I told myself that it didn't matter how far I strayed from God since I could just repent later and my sins would be forgiven. The further I drifted from God, the less conviction I felt. Soon, I hardly even cared how lost I was. One thing led to the next, and before I knew it, I was ditching class to get high, stealing alcohol, and taking the prescription medications I found in my house. After getting busted for possession of marijuana at school, I learned the hard way that the Lord chastens those whom He loves.

Getting kicked out of high school turned my whole world upside down. No more friends, no more freedom. Living on lockdown, I began to think of myself as worthless, a stain on our family's otherwise pristine image. Even though I tried to gain back my parent's trust, I constantly fell short and would beat myself up for letting them down time and time again. At a certain point, I stopped caring about being a letdown and accepted that I was a failure in their eyes. I stubbornly resisted my parent's influence on my decisions and chased my own desires until the time came for me to apply to college. University of California, Santa Barbara, had been my dream school since I was fifteen. I made school my first priority to improve my chances of getting in. The day that my letter from the UCSB Office of Admissions came in the mail, I mustered up a prayer to tell God that whether or not I had been accepted I would trust in His will for my life. Lo and behold, I made the cut. For the first time in my life, I felt like I had actually accomplished something significant and that my parents were proud of me.

When I first arrived at UCSB in 2011, the allure of Isla Vista attracted me for all the wrong reasons. Living away from home was as fun as I could have imagined, but the consequences of my actions quickly caught up with me. After my first couple of months of college, I had already been hospitalized for alcohol poisoning, thrown in the drunk-tank, and kicked out of the dorms. Having to move out of the dorms meant leaving behind the only place I felt like I really belonged. All of a sudden, I was alone in a new living situation and restricted from stepping foot inside the dorms, where all of my friends lived. In the midst of all of this, I was struggling to maintain a long-distance relationship with my girlfriend, which grew worse and worse throughout the year, until it was too volatile to work things out. After we broke up, I felt like I lost the only person who cared about me. At the time, I didn't realize how serious my self-destructive tendencies had become, as I spiraled deeper into drug and alcohol abuse than ever before. There were times when I thought I would rather die than deal with the comedowns and feelings of despair. I didn't believe that I deserved Jesus' help to pull me out of this slump. I had gotten myself into it, and I felt alone in trying to work my own way out of it. Over the next year, I struggled with depression and the use of drugs and alcohol as coping mechanisms to help me forget how worthless I felt. No matter how hard I tried, nothing seemed to work.

On the night of my twentieth birthday, I had a supernatural experience with the Lord that would change the course of my life. I had just made it back to my friend's house as things were winding down after a night of partying.

As I stepped into the bathroom, I heard a voice coming from within the wall ask me, "What do you think you're doing?"

At first I was terrified, but when I looked up to the source of the voice, I saw Jesus emerge from out of the wall before me, glowing radiantly with a heavenly crown atop His crown of thorns.

I heard Him tell me, "You've been blessed so rich-ly with a loving family, the opportunity to go to a great school, and a mind unlike any other. God has amaz-ing plans for you, but you're about to lose everything you care about in life if you don't change your ways."

I had been trying to hide from God long enough, trying to hide the fact that deep down in my heart I knew that I didn't love myself enough to care that I was ruining my life. I had been in denial for so long that I just kept digging deeper and deeper to hide what I had become from God. At that moment, it was as if I had just been yanked up out of the hole I dug and exposed to the light. As I stood there in His presence, eyes closed and head bowed, I felt the shame and fear inside of me disappear. I broke down sobbing as I felt how much God still loved me even though I had strayed so far from Him.

Overwhelmed with compassion, I responded, "I am so sorry. Can I please just have a hug?"

I heard him say, "Of course you can have a hug." As I reached out to embrace Him, I felt my heart explode with the warmth of His love and spread throughout my whole body.

"Open your eyes," He told me, "Look at yourself." I looked down to see that I was hugging myself.

"You need to learn how to love yourself before you can truly love others."

His words struck me to the core. My whole life I had tried to love others without ever learning how to love myself, but that night became the pivotal turning point in my walk with the Lord.

After that encounter, I started taking better care of myself and spending more time in prayer, reflect-ing on life and the decisions I had made. The mo-ment I humbled myself before God and asked for

His forgiveness, I realized that He had been watching over me all along, just waiting for me to reach out to Him. I decided that I was done letting drugs have any influence in my life; but during the time that I was mellowing out, there was a war going on for my mind. Nightmares haunted my sleep, robbing me of my peace of mind and instilling me with fear. I was afraid that I had strayed too far to make it back in one piece; I would never be the same again.

I was afraid that I had stumbled for too long to be worthy of God's grace. The lies of the enemy were taking their toll, and I needed to talk to someone I could trust. When I couldn't handle the ongoing spiritual conflict on my own anymore, I asked my parents for help. My mom called around, desperately trying to find a local pastor in the area who could help me through the turmoil. The first three people she talked to told her to contact Jason Lomelino, the pastor of Isla Vista Church. In the words of one local pastor, "He's seen more spiritual warfare than anyone I know. Whatever's going on, Jason can handle it." My mom contacted Jason, and the next day he called me and asked if I would like to come to Prayer & Prophecy on Monday night. Not really sure what to expect, I brought a friend with me, and we both ended up encountering the Holy Spirit through prophecy for the first time.

As we walked into the IV House of Prayer, we were welcomed by a couple of the friendliest strangers we had ever met. That night, I tangibly felt the presence of God. A peaceful essence rested in the midst of the people gathered in that room. I could see the light in their eyes, feel their compassion in the way they smiled, and I knew deep down that this was the real deal. When it was my turn to be prayed for, I introduced myself to Annalisa, Ava, Tarra, and Derrin. The words that they spoke gave me hope and erased any sliver of doubt that God still loved me. I didn't need to earn or deserve His affection. I only needed to accept it and let the Holy Spirit work in my life.

One prophetic image has resonated in my mind to this day. "I see a tree," Derrin said, "standing alone on top of a hill, completely barren without any leaves or fruit. All of a sudden, a lightning bolt struck it, and it burst forth with life, bearing fruits that dropped from the branches and rolled down the hill to plant new trees." In that moment, I no longer felt alone or worthless. I was filled with peace and joy as the Holy Spirit overcame me. I could feel God smiling down on me as I realized that my story could bring hope to others who struggled with the same problems I had once dealt with on my own.

During the next few months, the truth I learned about my identity in Christ completely reformed my perspective on what it means to have a relationship with the Lord. Romans 8 says,

"There is now no condemnation for those who are in Christ Jesus . . . and if the Spirit of Him who raised Jesus from the dead is living in you, He who raised Christ from the dead will also give life to your mortal bodies because of the Spirit who lives in you."

The words of hope in this chapter were the catalyst for a new season of redemption in my life. As soon as I realized that there was nothing that could stand between Jesus and I, my passion for Him became personal—and I would never be the same. There is no room for doubt or fear in a relationship with Jesus. Now that I've put all of my faith in God, I know that my life rests in the same hands that created our entire universe.

Over the past couple of years I've continued to be a part of Isla Vista Church, and now I even have the privilege of living in the Jesus Burgers house. Being a part of the IVC family as God's plan unfolds in Isla Vista has given me the opportunity to show God's love to others the same way it was shown to me. Praying for people and sharing my testimony has even led to some of my closest friends being saved. Before I came to Isla Vista Church, I didn't know that anybody still sought the spiritual gifts of healing and prophecy in today's society. Hearing people my age delivering prophetic words and healing in the name of the Holy Spirit opened my eyes to God's bound-less power over us and His love for the lost.

One evening as I was sitting by the fire at the Jesus Burgers house, one of the local homeless guys rode up on his bike. We invited him to come hang out with us. Lee had recently been saved, and as a new believer he was grateful beyond measure for God's grace in his life. After a while, he mentioned that he was suffering from arthritis in his knees, which made riding his bike painful. We asked if we could pray for him to be healed, and he agreed to give it a try.

We laid hands on him and prayed, "Lord, I thank you for Lee and how much You love him. We ask that You would heal his knees and get rid of any arthritis in his joints. Pain be gone in Jesus' name. Amen."

Lee stood up and walked around a little bit and bent down to test it out, but his knees still hurt.

"Okay, let's give it another try." I laid hands on his knees and said another prayer. This time, as he bent down to test it out, I saw his face light up in wonder. By the time he stood up out of his chair, his knees were no longer swollen, and he said they felt like new. We were in awe that God had just healed this man before our eyes. It's times like these that God restores our childlike faith in Him.

Since this day, Lee and I have become close friends, sharing stories of our redemption by the power of God's love. According to Jesus' teaching in Luke 7:41–50, those who once carried greater debts are the most grateful once forgiven. Jesus' sacrifice redeemed even the lowliest of sinners without exception, meaning that nobody is outside the reaches of His forgiveness. Even when we feel like we aren't worth being saved, God's infinite love bridges the gap and meets us in our times of need, bringing us hope out of despair and love out of fear.

MORE THAN
OKAY

LAUREN GREN

It was Christmas day. My dad and I were driving
home from spending the holidays with my grandparents, and he told me he was leaving my mom.
At eight-years-old, I vividly remember my first re-
sponse being, "It's okay."

I had tears streaming down my face, I felt nothing
but sadness, confusion, anger, and guilt, and the only
words I could utter were, "It's okay. I'm okay." I don't
know why I wasn't honest with my dad about how
I really felt, but something in my young, innocent
heart wanted to believe that I actually was fine. As I
repeated this to myself over and over again, I remember putting up an immediate wall, a wall that said I'm
never getting too close with anyone because they will
leave me and they will hurt me. This new wall I put
up became my shield, and with my shield in hand I
could convince my dad, myself, and this world that
Lauren was strong, Lauren was resilient, Lauren was
okay. As life progressed and troubles arose, I chose to
ignore the crap and cling even tighter to my shield,
to be focused and consumed with being okay. I kept
people just close enough so they wouldn't know that

inside I was actually the farthest thing from it.

I thought I would be able to be strong forever. I thought that I could ignore any tug on my heart, any soft spot coming, and that no person, no circumstance, nothing in this world would break me. Within those ten years, I constantly felt the pull of Jesus, a soft, but oh-so-persistent voice that said, "I will never leave." I recognized that voice because I used to know it. When my parents were together, I went to church and honestly believed God was a good Father and a Father who was always present. As soon as my earthly dad left I no longer believed He was for me. I no longer believed He loved me. How could a good Father do this? Why would He do this if He loved me? What could a little girl do to deserve this? As these questions permeated my mind, bitterness grew. Although my shield was made up of sadness, anger, fear, and now bitterness, there were moments I still felt the love of Jesus. I could feel His love fight through my walls and penetrate my heart. I didn't want this. I didn't want to feel this love because I knew it had the potential to destroy the hard, numb, strong persona I had worked to maintain. In all honesty, I was afraid of His love, I was terrified that His love would open my heart, just to break it all over again.

I got a phone call from my dad that said he was going to be getting a second divorce. Again, my first words were, "It's okay." Inside I was so hurt, so frustrated, so confused, it was as if all the pain from the first divorce came back up and was multiplied by two. Because I was supposed to be the strong girl, I had to put on an even stronger image after this divorce. I no longer had to be okay; I had to be great. I had to convince everyone around me that I was solid. This looked like me being extremely extroverted, loud, and social; being involved with youth groups, going on missions trips, and even doing a discipleship school in Mexico for six months. If people thought I was close to God, they wouldn't think I was a broken mess inside. In these following years, I experienced God in different ways. He never wasted these moments, even though I did it for selfish reasons. There were times I began to see the goodness of God. However, these glimpses didn't propel me to Him; they left me feeling out of control and scared. When I encountered God, I felt my strong girl image start to melt away. I felt my heart soften towards Him. So I stopped myself. I closed that door. I picked up my shield. This stubborn girl wouldn't let God back in that easily.

Three years passed as I went through life like this. In 2013, I visited my stepsister, Krissy (from my dad's second marriage), in Isla Vista. Visiting her was almost a joke; we probably had a total of five conversations together amidst our parents' seven years of marriage. But I hung out with Krissy and all of her friends and partook in Upper Room and Jesus Burgers.

In that trip, I decided I wanted to move here. Looking back now, I can say that God put this desire in me because He desperately wanted to give me a safe, Christian community that allowed me to be weak and vulnerable, and to uncover my breaking eight-year-old's heart. God is sneaky. I didn't know that was His plan. All I knew was I wanted out of my small town. I wanted to get away. I was tired of trying so hard to convince my closest family and friends that I was okay. I talked to Jason, and after a series of conversations and another visit, I was signed up to live at the Jesus Burgers house in September 2013.

The day I signed the lease, things started to shake. A huge amount of fear came as I decided to live in the Jesus Burgers house—fears of not being good enough, fears of being known, fears of being weak, and fears of not being okay. As these fears came up, I felt a loss of control. I couldn't control these fears and emotions, so I started to control something much more present. The day I arrived home from my vacation, I slowly became entangled in an "eating thing."

To therapists, friends, family and the world, I suffered with anorexia and bulimia. However, having an eating disorder by default means you're not okay, so to this day I call it an eating thing. I arrived in Santa Barbara with my eating thing, a bunch of walls and fears, a broken heart, a hard exterior, and absolutely no hope for anything better.

The first couple months were awful. I mean, awful. I wanted out. I hated it. I hated church and Jesus Burgers and affection and attention, and there were multiple times I just wanted to run. I did my best to wrap these emotions up in a pretty little bow. When people asked me how I was doing, I said everything is great, "I'm okay." I was hoping my short answers and isolation would keep people away. Not because they weren't genuine, amazing people, but because I felt like I was losing control of every aspect of my life. Although I did my best to push, shove, and resist people, they continued to pursue me. They weren't afraid of my walls; they fought against my isolated, cold, hard heart and still declared me enjoyable, beautiful, and lovable.

This constant love left me with one question: "Would they still love me if they knew I was so broken and the furthest thing from okay?" Through a period of time, that question was answered. Yes, they would love me through the mess and the pain. As people loved me and walked with me through this journey, I started to become even more real with others and more importantly, real with God. I started to have moments of honesty and vulnerability that I had never experienced before. As I slowly (and I mean, very slowly) started opening up my heart to Him, I realized my problems and pain didn't scare Him and He wasn't running away from me. Not only was God staying right by my side, but He also gave me something that I lost thirteen years prior: hope.

God gave me such hope—a gentle, graceful, loving, reassuring hope that said, "I love you. I have so much more in store for you. Days of joy, abundance, and ultimate freedom from every wall, every fear, and every insecurity await you. " It was with that truth that I was able to love and receive love from others in my house. That truth allowed me to look at people in the line at Jesus Burgers and say, I know life sucks, but I know, that I know, that I know, that there is so much more than this. There were many people I met while living at the Jesus Burgers house who said they just wanted to have fun and be happy, to disregard any pain and just be okay. Those thoughts couldn't make more sense to me. I know what it feels like to crave being okay. I listen, I fully understand, and I leave them with the same message I was given. Not some over the top, fake, joyful story that I fed to my family, friends, and peers for multiple years, but a message of hope, a message that simply says, "Jesus loves you and has so much more for you."

It's been nearly a year since I moved to this place, and let me tell you something, it's still really hard. I have had some incredible breakthroughs, some amazing conversations, some life-altering moments, but in all honesty, my first tendency is to grab my shield and push people away. When asked how I am or how my day was, I still smile and say, "Everything is okay!" I still struggle with wanting to control my emotions and my heart, and I'm still afraid of letting God into every aspect of my life. There's truly just one difference from a year ago to today, one thing that keeps me holding on, one thing that keeps me clinging, fighting, and searching for more of Jesus: hope. I don't know when the day will come when I experience the utter joy, abundance, and complete freedom that He's promised me, but it's coming. There is a day. Whether it's on earth or it's in heaven, there is a day. And until that day comes, I'm grasping onto the one thing that I couldn't be more sure of, I'm grasping onto Jesus. He is my only hope. He loves me. He is for me. He is never, ever leaving me. He has so much more in store for me.

SOMEONE
BETTER

LUCAS BELL

S omewhere between the age of nine and ten, a
deep longing in my heart told me that I was
ready to personally know Jesus. I vividly remember that evening, sitting at the dinner table with
my dad. I asked him, "How do you know Jesus?"

He proceeded to explain to me the prayerful process of letting Jesus into your heart. It was time to
make Jesus my own.

My parents had been Christians since I was one-
year-old. They were both radically saved out of the
New Age. My mom even went all over Montana, our
home state at the time, sharing her testimony at various churches because her story was so powerful. So
all of my life I have been going to church and culti-
vating a deep spiritual awareness. Even from a young
age, I have memories of being sensitive to God and
the spiritual realm. Growing up in this type of environment, I knew that Jesus was someone I wanted to
know, and in His divine timing He led me to Himself.

At the age of ten I moved to the East Coast, where
I attended a small, private Christian school. Attending
this school from sixth through twelfth grade gave me

an incredible foundation not only to know and pursue God but also to be launched into the pursuit of His Kingdom. My junior high and high school years were filled with Biblical teachings, encounters with God, outreach ministry, leadership training, an incredible group of friends, and a deep sense that God made me to change the world.

Upon graduating from high school, I moved to Santa Barbara, California. I had been accepted to Westmont College, a small, private Christian college in the foothills of Santa Barbara. This was the only school I applied to, and I knew without a doubt that God wanted me to go there. I didn't even bother to visit the campus. I just applied, got accepted, got on a plane, and showed up for freshmen orientation — naive, eighteen, and with the whole world in front of me. I had landed in the best place imaginable, and I was about to be shown a whole new aspect of the Kingdom of God. Among the many discoveries I had during my college years was the city of Isla Vista and the radiant community of Isla Vista Church.

My roommate, Trevor, forever one of life's dearest friends, invited me to join a small house church community in Isla Vista. He, his brother, and a few other friends decided they wanted to be intentional about pursuing family and Jesus together. At this point in my life, I was ready for a different expression of church. I felt strong in my faith, but I sensed that there was more to Christianity than the church was offering. Eagerly, I jumped into this house-church community. It felt like instant family. Every Thursday night, we would gather for dinner, prayer, sharing, discussion, and sometimes even dancing. I was blown away by this expression of church, the richness of the Holy Spirit's presence, and the deep friendships. In many ways I felt as if I were living the Book of Acts.

Several of these new friends also attended Isla Vista Church and invited me to attend various events. Upon recognizing the community's sincere love for Jesus and family, I was all in. Over the course of my four-year college career, I regularly visited Jesus Burgers, Isla Vista Church, and other weekly meetings. I began to form amazing relationships with the people there and helped out in different leadership capacities. By my senior year of college, I knew this was the family that I wanted to run with. I soon found myself dreaming of city transformation, creating movements, and growing a family of believers.

As I would frequently attend Upper Room and Jesus Burgers, I began to understand something about God and the expansion of His Kingdom: He wanted to change cities, and He wanted the hearts of the people in those cities. Now there is something very important to recognize about my story: I am a builder, innovator, and dreamer, but not necessarily an evangelist. However, you don't have to be an evangelist to participate in Jesus Burgers. You don't even have to be an evangelist to see people saved; you just have to be willing to love people and to follow God's leading. Over the years of attending Jesus Burgers, I enjoyed watching God move, observing people encounter Him, and the occasional prayer or prophetic time with a passer-by on the streets. I learned that Jesus Burgers was about loving people right where they are at and planting seeds into their spirits. I may not ever know the outcome of all the countless conversations and interactions, but God does, and He is faithful to capture His children's hearts with His love. I also integrated a mindset that I was going to be available and aware of what God is doing on the Jesus Burgers' nights. Over the years, these nights have been remarkable, full of faith, hope, and love manifesting. Our community could fill volumes of what God has done on these nights, but one story stands out in particular.

It was cold by the time we fired up the grill, but that didn't stop people from hitting the streets looking for the best party on this winter evening. I usually made it a habit to walk around the property and just check on everything. It was common for strangers to wander in the back of the Jesus Burgers house with masses of people always coming and going. As I made my usual rounds, I walked around the back corner of the house, and there was a shaggy blonde boy urinating on the back of the house—not an uncommon thing to happen in Isla Vista, but nonetheless inappropriate.

I quickly informed him of my presence as he finished his business.

He proceeded to ask me, "Do you have any weed?"

I responded, "No, I don't smoke weed, but I have something better."

Eagerly he asked, "What?"

"God!" I said.

"GOD? God has left me," he cynically remarked.

Immediately I said, "That's not who God is!"

I then began to explain to him who God is and how God is actually very close to him and loves him dearly. I apologized that he had been given a misrepresentation of God. And the next thing I knew, he was crying in my arms. He smelled heavily of alcohol, and it was obvious that he was not sober.

I asked him, "Would you like to know Jesus?"

Sobbing, he said, "Yes."

As I led him through a simple prayer and to the feet of Jesus, he began to sober up and come to his senses. Something in his eyes changed, and his heart was obviously in a soft, receptive place. I instantly

knew that his misunderstanding of God was causing him to feel alone, rejected, and abandoned in life.
By simply proclaiming the truth of who God is, a lie
broke off of his life, and he became positioned to encounter the Father.

After he came out of his salvation encounter, we
stood there in the back area of the house, just hugging and rejoicing. What an incredible moment! I
literally just watched a high, drunk kid get radically
touched by the love of God and enter the Kingdom of
Heaven. We proceeded to make our way to the front
of the house where the Jesus Burgers grilling was taking place, hoping to get a burger. However, the burgers were all gone, so I invited him to a late night sand-
wich at one of the local delis in Isla Vista. We hung
out for another hour while he told me his story. Due
to certain circumstances in his life, a false representation of God had been established in his heart. As
I listened to his story, I reaffirmed how deeply God
cared for him and had been with him the whole time.
In reality, he was just out partying that night looking for something to cure his pain, something better.
However, God had different plans for him as he indeed encountered Someone better. I told him about
our community and encouraged him to join us for
the Sunday gathering. He agreed avidly, wanting it all.

Although I never saw him again after that night, I
rode my bike home knowing something real had tak-
en place in his heart. I was ecstatic from his salvation
experience. If leading people to God was this good,
then I wanted more. Seeing a newborn come into the
Kingdom has to be one of the greatest moments of
a believer's life. No wonder evangelists are so on fire
to bring souls into the Kingdom; the experience is
absolutely remarkable. God's goodness and love will
abound in the midst of following the Holy Spirit.

Jesus Burgers is a place for people to encounter God through being tangibly loved. All I did that night was show my new friend that God loved him and that there was something better than alcohol and weed to make him feel high. His story is unique, but it shows that there are countless people who are looking for something better, for someone to tell them that they are loved by God and that they can experience the saving grace and freedom of salvation. Since this encounter, I have told myself that I may not be an evangelist, but I am capable of leading people to God. Because I know God, I am comfortable sharing my experience of Him with others. In this particular instance, I was put in front of someone who desperately needed his view of God changed. He may have heard of God, but he was unaware that God loved and cherished him despite all of his unfortunate circumstances in life. But that is how good God is. God, no matter what, always and unconditionally loves us.

GIVEN A
FUTURE AND
A HOPE

VICTORIA PEVARNIK

W hen I talk with people about Jesus, they sometimes ask me if I was raised Christian. "Not quite," is my usual answer. Thinking about who I am now and who I was before Jesus, I have to answer this way. The life that God planned for me is so much more beautiful than anything I was making of my life. He is the great giver of life, hope, and glorious futures, in spite of ourselves.

I grew up with some Catholic influence at home until my parents divorced when I was eight. I had an idea that there was a God, but the lack of mention of God affected me. As I got older, I easily accepted teachings of evolution and was very interested in watching movies like *The Craft* or playing with tarot cards and ouija boards. In middle school, I started smoking weed and drinking. With each grade level, I gained a new drug of choice: from painkillers to hallucinogens to stimulants. As I went into college, I was into the hippie and rave scenes. I spent every weekend at house parties, shows, or festivals. I sold drugs so I could extravagantly party, travel around the tri-state area, and get high enough to not remember anything after midnight. My heart wanted adventure and excitement, but I didn't know how to satisfy those desires with good things. In turn, the reality of my youth was this: by my freshman year in college, I was addicted to drugs and didn't see any hope for my future. Even though I graduated high school in the top 10 percent of my class, I dropped out of my first year of college twice, and by my sophomore year, I was strung out on heroin and cocaine. Soon I found myself in Las Vegas in a three-day, drug-induced coma.

My story could have ended there. I could have been like some of my friends who died from overdoses, ended up in jail, or lived with diseases. I could have left my parents with deep pain in their hearts for how my life ended. Everyone else would have just forgotten about me after some time. I would never have had the chance to have the life that I have now nor to play my part in this world. But that was neither the future nor the identity God had for me. When I was in that drug-induced coma, I encountered the Living God. I saw a vision of myself in restraints, unable to get out of them even though I was fighting them so strongly. Then I heard a voice say, "If you just let go, I will restore everything." I stopped fighting the restraints and began to see them being cut away. With each cut, I heard a word for what God would restore in my life: family, school, work, future . . .

Coming out of the coma, I didn't know what to make of the experience. I went to rehab and relapsed afterwards only to find myself in the same vicious cycle. I was fed up with my way of living and wanted out, but I just couldn't do it on my own. One day, a pastor and his wife drove two-and-a-half hours from a church in Philadelphia to tell me about Jesus. She shared with me how God had good plans for my life, and that in Him there is a future and a hope. She told me about Jesus's love for me and how through His forgiveness I was accepted by Him. Even though the lady sharing the Gospel with me only spoke Spanish and I was listening through a translator, my heart was stirred, and I believed in Jesus that day. After I prayed with her, things were not the same. Even though I tried for the next couple of weeks to get high, I couldn't feel that high anymore. God was supernaturally intervening in my life. I started to pray to God for help, and He began to answer me. I hungered even more for real change in my life. I was finally willing to surrender my ways of doing things and seek His guidance in my life. An opportunity for me to go into a Christian recovery ministry arose, and I took it. There, the truth of the Gospel, the forgiveness of all my past, and the great things that a life with God had in store for me were becoming a reality for me. I had finally found the one thing that brought real joy, adventure, and newness into my life.

God has done many wonderful things in my life since then, but my section of this book cannot contain them, so let's skip ahead. Nine years later, part of God's plan was to call my husband and pregnant self to the Santa Barbara area. We were at UC Irvine at the time. We met there at a campus outreach, fell in love, and got married. After getting married, we felt called to God's Kingdom work on college campuses in Southern California and amongst the youth. We were part of a few campus ministries at UCI and our church. While enjoying our time there, God spoke to us about moving—a year before we actually did. We had no idea what it was going to look like, where we were going, or why we were going, but we knew God was going to move us. We began to pray for direction.

After my husband finished grad school, God opened the door for a job at UCSB. It happened so fast that I left my job, packed everything in three weeks, and left all we knew in SoCal to come to Isla Vista. I was excited for new things, but I didn't know what to expect. We drove the streets of IV on a Saturday afternoon searching for an apartment. The residents began the usual long evening of partying, the yards filled with people, and the music began booming from balconies. When I saw this, I got more excited and filled with compassion. I wanted to move into this town so I could be among these people. Not unlike me in my youth, they were seeking hope, adventure, and life in the only way they knew how. I wanted them to know the power of the Risen Christ, who offers so much more than a good time. It was the middle of the quarter at UCSB, so it was hard to find a place in Isla Vista. We decided to move close by in Goleta, where we began to seek why God had moved us to this area.

We had four weeks before my due date to get settled in our new spot. It was intense unpacking, figuring out insurance and doctors, and getting used to a new town. While I was busy settling in, my husband went to work each day and continued to pray that God would connect us to a church family and speak to us about why we were here. God heard my husband's prayer. I decided to check out the local prayer houses, SBHOP and IVHOP. Through IVHOP we found Isla Vista Church and decided to go there our second Sunday in town. We walked into the church during worship, and the presence of God was very tangible. As we worshipped, Jesus began to speak to my husband and I. At the very same time, without us knowing it, Jesus broke our hearts for Isla Vista, for His people in the city, and for the people in His Church. After worship, Holly Lomelino shared her story on how, by faith, she dropped her plans and followed God's call to Isla Vista. This message hit home because it was so much like what we just did. It was sweet confirmation to our souls. We knew why God called us here: Isla Vista. Everyone in the church was very welcoming, and we were blessed to be a part of this family at such an important time of transition.

We were excited to see what God was doing in IV firsthand, so the next Friday night, we went to Jesus Burgers. We encountered God's presence at Upper Room and were excited to hit the streets and get around the people of this city. I wanted to love them and share my light with them. Nine months pregnant, with much supernatural grace, I stood by the sign that read "Holy Spirit Love Encounters," and prayed for people. My husband and I went to Jesus Burgers a couple of times before our daughter, Hope, was born. Soon after, we felt like we should move into Isla Vista; three months later, we did. When Jesus Burgers started for the next school year, my husband and I made it out as often as we could.

At Jesus Burgers, I love standing by the "Free Blessings" sign or in the street talking to people. It's definitely a great place to have direct conversations about God. During Deltopia, the second largest city-wide party in Isla Vista, the Holy Spirit's presence came strongly at the sign. We had been moving the Jesus Burgers' grill down Del Playa from house party to house party, serving burgers and loving people. At one point, I chatted with a young man who came up to the sign with his friend who was asking for a blessing. My prayer that day was to share the full Gospel message with someone. In the midst of thousands of partygoers who were on the move, I thought it would be a little challenging to get into a deep conversation. However, God thought it was easy.

In two minutes, I was able to share with him that

Jesus, God's Son, came to the earth to reveal God to us and then die in our place of punishment for our sins so we can be forgiven. Through His forgiveness, we are freed of guilt and restored to a new life that is lived in relationship with God, who loves us.

As he listened, I watched him realize what God did for him. Just before his friend beckoned him to leave the sign, the man looked at me with eyes that hungered for Jesus. He said, "Thank you for sharing this with me. I always wanted to know what the point of the cross really was. Now I know, and I believe." I will see him again in the Kingdom one day. In the midst of this crazy, drunken block party that later turned into a semi-violent riot making nationwide news, Jesus was calling His child home.

Even though some conversations with people on the streets during Jesus Burgers were a bit challenging, God always confirmed in my heart after leaving for the night that He was present in the situation and was working His love in people's hearts. Jesus said, "My Father is always at His work to this very day, and I too am working" (John 5:17). Just as God, through His relentless love, performed His saving, life-changing work in me, God is doing the same thing on the streets of Isla Vista and in all the earth. I am thankful that I get to see what He is doing here in IV, that this was part of His future for me, and that He gave me real hope for my life and for the lives of every person.

God gave me a little girl named Hope as a permanent reminder of the future that He had for me outside of the path I was on. Who would have thought I would be a physical and spiritual mother hoping for new life all around me? Thinking of this, I have pulled Hope in a wagon down the streets of Isla Vista as she waved and smiled to the students, giving them joy and a sense of hope for their futures as well.

FOREVER CHANGED

CARRIE MANSIS

I don't remember the day I gave my life to Jesus. For some people, that day is forever etched in their memory as the day God came in and changed their lives. But for me, I never knew life any other way. I was raised in a Christian home and, starting from a young age, I was involved with churches, Christian schools, and Bible camps before my small mind could even comprehend who God was. In some ways, being raised to know and love God was a blessing, because constantly learning about Him and being reminded of His presence in my life sealed in me a firm belief about how much He loves me and how real He is. On the other hand, as much of a blessing it was, being raised around "everything Christian" made being a Christian routine and insincere.

Going through life with these spiritual mindsets constantly intersecting resulted in my teenage and young adult years being metaphorically comparable to a swinging pendulum. The pattern was always the same. There would be a time when I was actively and happily engaged in a relationship with God, felt close and connected to Him, and trusted Him with my life, and things were good. Then, one way or another I would lose touch with Him and where He was in my life, I would slowly stop talking to Him, and my Bible would collect dust. I became more interested in other things and less interested in my relationship with Him. Weeks and months and sometimes years would go by before I came back to God, usually in moments of desperation, only to have the cycle repeat. When I was about nineteen, I had fallen away from God again, into a darkness beyond what I had experienced before.

At age thirteen, I was diagnosed with a retina disease that is very serious and unpredictable. My disease had been under control for some time, but when I was nineteen, it flared up again. Within days unexpectedly left me with permanent double vision, robbing me of what felt like everything at the time — the ability to drive, read, watch a movie, use a computer, enjoy a sunset, and so on. Even the most basic things like doing homework or reading PowerPoint lectures in class became a scene of frustration and tears. This situation left me angry and hopeless beyond words, thinking my life would never be the same. In addition to that, I had been seriously addicted to an online game on and off for three years prior, and as a result I let go of all my past friendships, successfully isolating myself beyond recognition. In my anger and loneliness, I was driven into a sadness that started out small but grew over months into a deep depression coupled with crippling anxiety. On days when I wasn't at school or work, I was at home, drowning in TV, video games, or books, always immersing myself in a different reality so I wouldn't have to think about my own.

Being depressed is a slow death. There were days when I felt fine, could laugh with my family at dinner, go for a walk, or run errands like anyone else. But other days I couldn't find a reason to go on. I remember days when I would wake up in the morning feeling angry because I wanted to still be sleeping, because sleeping was somewhere reality couldn't find me. Other days I couldn't sleep at all, too plagued with anxious thoughts, trying to find a way out, but getting nowhere. Expressing emotions was so strenuous and draining, almost like I didn't know how. First there would be nothing, and then all at once, everything. I would explode in fits of rage first, so much energy poured into anger and violence, fueled only by desperation, and then I would quickly fall into hopelessness and defeat.

As the depression grew deeper, I started thinking of death, wishing I would get into a fatal accident on the freeway or something. This progressed into thinking about suicide; first slowly, then eventually, until I thought about it every day. I struggled with these emotions and found twisted relief from them in self-harm. I couldn't see truth or hope. I was plagued with negative thoughts about myself and my future. Back then, I believed that there was nothing good in anything, there was nothing good about life, and there was nothing that was worth it. I thought that people who believed otherwise had fooled themselves and were living a lie. I saw no value in friendships, family, love, work, honor, pleasure, or anything else because it all led to the same end—you just die and your whole time on earth is hard and meaningless. And I was eager to get to that end, because I hated myself and hated my reality.

At the apex of these struggles, it came time for me to transfer to UCSB. Even though Santa Barbara was less than two short hours from my hometown outside of Los Angeles, I was pretty afraid of what would become of me in this new environment. I was already suffering from an anxiety disorder, and I feared that in my delicate inner state I literally might not make it. During the first week of school, there were tons of activities going on. All the campus organizations provided opportunities to get connected. Without really thinking about it, I ended up going to a social event for a Christian group on campus. While it was awkward at first, I ended up being introduced to a girl named Michelle, and we got into more of a serious conversation. Before I knew it, she was telling me things about my life that I had not told anyone for years. Sheaid that God had a radical plan of healing and growth for my life in the coming year. After we said our goodbyes, I called my mom right away and talked to her for an hour about how amazing my evening was. I was suddenly filled with a glimmer of hope for my future after being reminded that God had never stopped caring for me and never gave up on His plans for my life.

Not long after, Michelle invited me to a Bible study for Isla Vista Church. I didn't know anything about IVC, but I met some great people in the Bible study who got me connected with the church. One of the girls, Bre, even took me under her wing and spiritually encouraged me in all things. She invited me to church and met up with me often to talk about Jesus and how to hear His voice in my life.

Around the same time, a few friends of mine who didn't go to IVC invited me to Upper Room and Jesus Burgers. We got to Upper Room a little late, so the place was full and people were already worshipping. I found a seat in the back and observed, because I didn't know any of the words to the songs they were singing. I remember seeing one girl sing and dance like no one was watching. She looked so free, and it was clear to anyone who looked at her that she was truly focused completely on Jesus in that moment. I envied her freedom and joy. No sooner had I thought that when her eyes, which were closed, popped open and stared directly at me. Then she came right over to me and introduced herself as Annalisa. She said she wanted to pray for me and that she heard God tell her a few things about me that she wanted to share. She began praying and prophesying over me. Within minutes I was huddled over sobbing, while she addressed so many of my fears and past hurts that I was afraid to bring before God. She continued to press on in prayer despite my breakdown. When we were done, I felt exhausted from the release of all the emotions and burdens I had been carrying around with me for years.

After Upper Room, we got into a conversation about what we just prayed about, and what I was currently going through. When it came time to leave, we said goodbye. I walked home with my friends in total shock of what had just happened. God was clearly reaching out to me in so many ways, through all the people I was meeting and all the things they were saying. The anxiety and depression I had was being cast out as I inched closer to God. He loved me so much that He was cloaking me in His light, lifting the burden of those things so that I could see my future in Him. I decided I would respond to God's call and continue going to where He was leading me. At the time, that looked like going to IVC and the IVC Bible study, a Christian club on campus, and Jesus Burgers. My time was filled to the brim with all things God; I was so hungry for His presence and for Him to move in my life. I began forming friendships at these places and learning more about hearing God's voice, and I started journaling and reading my Bible constantly. I was completely committed, devoted, and invested in God.

Before long, I decided that I wanted to live in the Jesus Burgers house. When the time rolled around for me to move in, I was beyond excited, the happiest I had been in my young adult life. The first few months were absolute bliss. I loved my housemates and the fellowship we had with each other. I loved that people felt safe in our home and knew it was somewhere they were always welcome. Each day was a new adventure with God.

One night at Jesus Burgers, I ended up talking with a girl from Sweden. She was moved by what we were doing at Jesus Burgers every Friday night. We struck up a conversation, and she shared more about her life and her past. I got to see her again and again at Jesus Burgers. We got together for lunch, and she came to IVC a few times. She even had me over for dinner, where I met her roommate, who started coming to Jesus Burgers and hanging out at the house too. We were all becoming good friends, brought together just by God giving me the opportunity to hand her a simple burger one evening.

After a few months, one of the girls came to Jesus Burgers looking distressed. She was talking with a friend when I spotted her across the yard. All of a sudden, she burst into tears. She got up and walked around the house, trying to find a private area to weep. I quickly went over to her to see what had happened, but it took her so long to get any words out between sobs. I invited her upstairs, and we sat in my bedroom for a long time before any words were spoken. We got to talk for over an hour about her life and her relationship with God. I shared some of my story with her too. Although nothing crazy or supernatural happened that night, I was able to experience the absolutely glorious gift of relationship that God has given us.

As we sat there together crying and sharing hard things in our lives, I realized that sometimes the best way to comfort and love someone is simply by being there to listen, to let them know they are fully heard by someone, and more importantly, by God. Sometimes we get caught up in thinking our lives are insignificant and our problems are trivial compared to other things going on around us, or that our lives are doomed to be hard and meaningless. But God sees every detail of our lives, knows our every thought, happy or sad, feels every tear, and cares about the cause of every single one. He is next to us at every moment, opening doors for us, pulling us away from danger, and loving us to an unlimited capacity every day. My friend left that Friday still believing and declaring that God loved her, and that she loved Him. Though she didn't figure it all out in one night, she chose to believe in the truth that nothing will ever separate us from God's love (Romans 8:38–39).

As the year progressed, I found myself facing more and more challenging circumstances and feelings. I even fell back into some of my old thoughts and habits. I am still walking through some of those things today, but I know I'm not on that pendulum anymore. My life has been forever changed by Jesus and His abundant love for me. I know that without a doubt God cares for me deeply and has a plan for my life. He won't abandon me. And He feels the same way about you, too. I want to face each day like my friend: no matter what is going on in my heart, I will always believe in and declare the power of God's love.

GOD'S
PROMISE

LINDSAY BELT

It was 2007; I had just graduated high school, was "figuring out my life" (as most people claim at that age), and was in a very unhealthy relationship with a boy. I was running from everything that was truth in my life up until that point. My family, my friends, and even my god at that time were all letting me down, so I was determined to run the other way.

It wasn't until years later that I realized who God truly is, where He was during all these hard times, what He had planned for me, and how He wanted to fulfill promises in my life. Jesus Burgers played a big step in that process. As our ministry affected my life and helped others discover their purpose, it helped me in finding mine.

In the middle of 2008, I went to Maui, Hawaii, on a Discipleship Training School with YWAM (Youth With A Mission) and also on an outreach to Thailand and Nepal. The experiences and the adventures I had in these different places were so surreal and exciting, and I saw God in a tangible way, but for some reason it just wasn't enough. I didn't physically feel Him like I knew I wanted to or expected to.

A few years later, I was still in my horribly unhealthy relationship and still questioning my identity.
I was constantly fighting with my boyfriend. He was
lying to me over and over, and I had accepted every lie
because I thought I would never find someone better or know anything different. No matter how low
I felt or whatever "love" I accepted, God knew my
identity and what I was made for. He began speaking
to me again, and I finally decided to listen. I would
write down—day after day, month after month—all
the little words that God was speaking into my life as
He shaped my identity through them. What stood out
the most was, "The moment you let go of him is the
moment I will give you something greater." I always
knew that God was telling me I had to let go of this
relationship, I had to let go of this man, and I had to
get healing for my heart so He could prepare me for
someone better. But I ignored Him. I could only see
through my fogged-up glasses what was right in front
of me, rather than God's greater picture for my life.

In January of 2011, I made my first trip to Santa
Barbara, California. My cousin and my aunt lived
there, and I desperately needed any excuse to get
away from my hometown and the life I was living. It
was only for a couple of days, but it was enough to
make me fall in love with the city and all its beauty.
I instantly knew I had to come back. So, I did. Every
couple of weeks I would make the three-and-a-half-
hour drive to Santa Barbara and stay with my cousin
and her roommates. On one of my trips there, her
roommates invited me to this church called Isla Vista
Church. They told me I would love it, there were tons
of people my age, and they were all on fire for God in
the way that I absolutely longed to be. So, I went to
this little church in this little town where people were
passed out on the streets and there was throw up on

the sidewalk. I truly could not have felt more at home.

Walking into the church was like walking into a party! Everyone knew each other by name. Guys and girls alike were hugging and genuinely expressing their love for one another. I knew that I had to be part of this. During my first experience there, I sat down in a pew by myself in order to really let the service sink in. Midway through the worship set, a woman named Marilynn came up to me without hesitation and told me that I had a specific purpose in this church. She said I was supposed to be there and that I was going to be used in a huge way there. Lastly, she gave me permission to pray for people and speak into their lives. I was pleased and thankful that someone had even noticed me, let alone took the time to tell me all these amazing things. Yet, I didn't believe anything she said because I still didn't feel good enough. Little did I know, she would become one of the most influential people in my life, someone who has actually helped me grow into the woman I am now.

That first experience with this hippie little church, where everyone dressed casually and danced around and had a ton of fun, made me realize it was supposed to be my home! In one church service, God had planted seeds of identity and promise in me. I told the Lord that day that if He allowed me to move to IV, I was going to dedicate my life to that church.

And He did just that. He gave me a home in Isla Vista, and He helped me fulfill my dreams and realize the promises He gave me. I rededicated my life to the Lord and was baptized in front of my family and friends. I had finally felt the sense of deep love and connection that I had been longing for the last few years. It wasn't until 2013 that I finally understood what God was telling me those years before, "The moment you let go of him is the moment I will give you something greater." God was giving me Himself in exchange for the horrible relationship I was in. I was excited to receive Him as my greatest gift. That same month I decided to live in a rather small space with five girls I didn't know. I was forced to really seek after all He had for me. I knew authentic community was something I had been longing for, so I pursued it.

Just by witnessing the love and friendship within the community at IVC, I was changed and able to accept my identity. I knew that Jesus Burgers was causing an outpouring of God's love through our body onto this awesome city of Isla Vista and helping others to receive their true identity and calling as well.

God had made so many promises to me, and I knew that this was a year of fulfillment. By September, I was fully in the swing of things, living with these amazing girls whom I now love so much. God had been redeeming my soul over and over again and had really restored my heart. When October and November rolled around, I slid back into some old patterns. I started dating a guy. I thought this would be a good idea and something that I could have control over, but the truth was that I knew nothing would survive in my life unless God had full control. Sadly, I still chose to take matters into my own hands. I went home for Thanksgiving break to see my family, and my new boyfriend and I fell right back into where I was years before. He and I slept together. I knew instantly in my heart this was not where I wanted to be or where I was meant to be. That night we ended things, and I knew that I had been redeemed and was going to follow after God with my whole heart.

That night changed my life entirely. On the morning of December 23, 2013, I went to work not feeling myself, and my boss jokingly told me to go to the store and take a pregnancy test. I laughed it off because three years earlier my doctor had told me there was a very low chance I would ever become pregnant due to a syndrome I had. As I sat there in the back room at work, I began to pray. God reminded me, "I promised you that you would be a mother." I ran across the parking lot not willing to take a chance any longer and proceeded to take the test. At 6:42 a.m. in the back room at Starbucks, the word "PREGNANT" turned pink across the screen. My heart sank to the floor. I began to weep. I knew that this was going to be a year of fulfilled promises, but never in a million years did I expect that kind of promise. A flood of emotions took over my body, and I couldn't even speak out words. The only thing I knew was: I am going to be a mother. God was fulfilling His promises and my identity in a way I could never have expected.

The next day was Christmas Eve, and my parents were on their way to Santa Barbara to have dinner with me and my roommates. As my parents arrived, my fear and excitement were competing for space in my thoughts. My mom walked in and immediately set out on her cooking adventure for the evening, while my heart continued to pound out of my chest. I knew I had to tell her that instant, or I would explode with every emotion possible. I began to weep as I told her what I had done and what was to come out of it. After minutes that felt like years of tears and hugs and my mom continually telling me how much she loved me, my dad walked in. My mom proceeded to share the news with him. My father, the man whom I looked up to in every way possible, whom I was so fearful to tell, looked down at me and with a grin on his face said to me, "Oh, honey, I love you so much. You will be a great mother. We will get through this." From that point on, I knew I was going to have nothing but love and support from everyone around me. The next step was to tell my other family, Isla Vista Church. They set out to love and accept people every Friday night at Jesus Burgers, but could they accept me too?

I knew that God had promised to use me in a huge way in this congregation, so I had to trust Him in that. Later that week, after the holidays had settled, I sat down with my pastor and friend, Jason Lomelino, and poured my heart out about what was going on in my life. He smiled, was completely open to listening, and made me feel worthy. He didn't look at me as though he were staring at the sin. He had looked at me like Jesus would, loving me regardless of the sin, and loving and accepting the child growing inside of me. Jason willingly walked me through some of the hardest months of my life and showed me my true identity in Christ apart from my sin.

Shortly after, I stood in front of the church one Sunday afternoon and told my story. I didn't start with exclaiming what a sinner I was or condemning myself. I simply stood there, completely fearful and vulnerable, laying my heart out on the line. This was the time when God really showed me what this church was all about: love. I shared with them, my family, my friends, and even a ton of strangers who were visiting our church for the first time, what I was genuinely going through and what I needed from them.

I told them, "I'm not condoning or condemning what I did, but I am asking, because God calls us to do this for our family, for love and support from all of you. I am going to need a lot of practical help and encouragement through this transition in my life, and I'm asking you to please stand with me."

As I looked up at the church through my tear-stricken eyes, one by one everyone stood to their feet in agreement with me, applauding what I had placed before them. I knew that I would be okay. I knew that God would guide me through this, and I knew, above all else, that I had family and friends to fully rely on through these next few months and even for the rest of my life. God didn't let me down then, and He continues to keep me going even now. As I continued to go to church and Jesus Burgers, I was able to use my amazing testimony to uplift people and encourage them that there is light, love, and acceptance in the midst of whatever sin they are in.

I wouldn't have my life any other way. I know God has me in His hands and is continually guiding and leading me down His path for my life. God promised us that our city, Isla Vista, will be His. I can rightfully say His promises will be fulfilled and Isla Vista will be touched and moved by His love through Jesus Burgers, through IVC, and through my family there. I am naming my daughter Iris, which means *rainbow* in Greek, to signify God's promises in my life. I cannot wait for Iris to see a city changed and moved by the love of God and the love of His children. He, my greatest gift, has given me this identity and promise, and I am blessed to journey on with Him.

3

Love

Love bears all things, believes all things,
hopes all things, endures all things.

1 Corinthians 13:7 (ESV)

LOOKING
FOR LOVE

AMANDA OLSON

For years I lived a life of drugs, alcohol, boys, and whatever else my flesh desired. My parents divorced shortly after they had me, and my mother remarried when I was seven. As a little girl, I lived two lives: one during the week with my mom and stepdad and one during the weekend with my dad. Although my mom rarely talked about religion, my father always took me to church. I still remember jumping up and down as a little girl in my dad's van as he turned into the church parking lot every Sunday morning. The pure and innocent joy I felt for the Lord at a young age was short lived.

Living two lives and going back and forth between broken families was incredibly confusing and hard as an only child. Although I had every material thing a young girl could ever want, I was ungrateful, rebellious, and self-absorbed. In my adolescent years, I regularly shoplifted food, jewelry, clothing, and whatever else satisfied the temporary rush I got from breaking the law. I screamed at my parents, fought with my stepdad, wrote profane words on our home's walls, and ran away countless times. My rebellion caused my parents tears, sweat, and pain. I fantasized of a day when I would fall in love with a boy, run away with him, and have a family of my own. When I think of it all now, I giggle at my childish foolishness; but this was the reality of my adolescent years. I was lost, broken, angry, and looking for love. In high school, I boldly labeled myself an "atheist." Although my dad took me to church when I was younger, my broken heart, suicidal thoughts, and extreme depression caused me to believe that if God did exist, He surely did not care enough about me to fix my family. When I was fifteen, a friend's boyfriend introduced me to marijuana. Many say it is impossible to become physically addicted, but I quickly became mentally addicted. Marijuana let me escape from my reality and made me feel rebellious and carefree.

Throughout my teenage years, I would often sneak out of my house in the wee hours of the night to smoke marijuana with boys who never had my best interest in mind. Even though I never physically engaged with them, I loved the fact that they desired and craved my beauty. It made me feel powerful, appreciated, and most of all, it was the closest thing I felt to love. But the attention I received from boys was never enough. There was always still something missing in my heart, and I always knew it.

My senior year, I enrolled in class at the community college near my house. I made a friend in the class who started telling me about Jesus. He informed me that his dad had just passed away, but despite this, he had hope in the living God. To be honest, I kind of thought my friend was a little crazy at first, but I quickly realized there was something really different about this friend. In fact, the hope he carried was so foreign to me that I became curious to know why he seemed so different than anyone I had ever met.

This was the first time someone talked to me about Jesus. I was intrigued and wanted to know more. Then I met his friends. They went to a neighboring high school and spent weekends consuming copious amounts of alcohol, abusing drugs, and having unprotected sex. I quickly became friends with them and forgot about the hope my friend had given me.

A few days before my eighteenth birthday, my mother informed me that I needed to live somewhere else. The anger, hurt, depression, and abuse in our home was too much for her to handle, and either my stepdad or I needed to temporarily leave. Looking back, I understand my mother's decision, but at the time I felt angry and betrayed. I started to believe the lie that she loved my stepdad more than she loved me.

For six months, I lived with a friend and her father a few miles away from my mom's home. I spent the last days of my senior year continuing to look for love and acceptance in drugs and alcohol at raves and house parties. A few months later, I was accepted into UCSB, and my mother and I started to reconcile our relationship. She offered to help finance my tuition if I would move back in with her. A top-ranked university and a party school right on the beach—it seemed like the perfect fit for me.

I moved to UCSB with my belongings and the emotional baggage I had carried around in high school. Though my mother supported me going to UCSB in hopes that I'd get an education, I was too focused on other things to appreciate her incredible sacrifices. Rather than concentrating on my studies, I continued looking for love through drugs, parties, and of course, boys. Not surprisingly, nothing seemed to fill the hole in my heart. After two quarters of failing grades at the university, I was dismissed with a 1.98 GPA. Devastated and depressed, I attended community college the spring quarter of my freshman year and was readmitted into the university that summer. I often contemplated whether God was real or not, but I always had more doubt than faith. So I continued my lifestyle of drinking and doing drugs. This time around, I felt emptier than I ever had. In fact, I had never felt so empty in my life.

On Halloween weekend, a friend asked me if I wanted to try hallucinogenic mushrooms with him. With no hope, no goals, and no purpose in my life, I quickly accepted the invitation. It was October 26, 2013, and I remember the experience more vividly than any other experience in my life. As my trip began, my body and mind started to feel drastically different. My friend asked if I wanted to walk around Isla Vista. As we were walking, my mind was captivated by God's creation. I couldn't understand how the world was so beautiful, but I knew there was no way it was accidentally so perfect. I realized that all the times I contemplated God's existence, He had been pursuing me. As we walked down the infamous party street, Del Playa, we approached a large and wide gravel path that runs along the bluffs; it was a path I had run on countless times. As we walked on the wide path, one of my friends found a narrow path to the side and jokingly asked me if I wanted to "go down the narrow path" with him. Although I didn't understand it at the time, the words vividly stuck out in my mind.

As the hallucinogens started to wear off, I began to feel depressed and wanted to be alone, so my friend took me back to my house. I instantly fell on my bedroom floor and started weeping louder than I have ever wept in my life. I wept for all the times I disobeyed and dishonored my parents. I wept for all the times I delighted in getting attention from a boy to satisfy my own insecurity. I wept for anything I had ever stolen, for every girl I ever condemned with my tongue, and for all the times that I had looked for love in everything except the Creator, Love Himself.

As my tears came to a slow cease, I started praying. I had only prayed once in my life before this day. "God, if you're real and you love me like people have told me, would you reveal yourself to me? God, I promise I will give my life to you if you are real!" I cried out to the Lord and suddenly felt an overwhelming desire to read the Bible, despite the fact I had read only one or two verses of the Bible before. I knew I needed to read God's word, but I didn't have a Bible! However, I did know about the Christian website Biblegateway. I prayed again and asked God to speak to me. "God, if you are real, then give me a verse and speak!"

I heard a voice in my head say, "Matthew 7." I typed "Matthew 7" into the search bar and read,

"Ask and it will be given to you; seek and you will find; knock and the door will be opened to you. For everyone who asks, receives; the one who seeks, finds; and to the one who knocks, the door will be opened."

The words spoke right to me! God had just revealed Himself to me! As if that wasn't enough, I went on to read more and started weeping tears of joy as I read Matthew 7:13–14,

"Enter through the narrow gate. For wide is the gate and broad is the road that leads to destruction. But small is the gate and narrow is the way that leads to life, and there are few who find it."

I instantly thought back to my friend asking me if I wanted to walk down the narrow path with him, and I knew God was clearly answering my prayer in ways

I would know He is real.

God is real! I was in so much shock. What do you do when the Creator of the universe reveals Himself to you? I thought people would think I was crazy from the hallucinogens, but I knew one friend would believe me. Lizzy had been messaging me for weeks, asking me question after question about God, debating His existence with me. I told her what had happened. She was in as much shock as me! She continued asking me questions I had no idea how to answer. The only answer I knew was: God is REAL!

So I prayed. I prayed that God would put me in a loving community of believers to help spread His love in this city. God highlighted Isla Vista Church, and I started going out to Jesus Burgers winter quarter of my sophomore year. I felt a little strange when I first started going to Jesus Burgers. I felt hypocritical because only weeks before I had been partying with the same people I was now sharing the Gospel with. But that's the thing—God's love is so good, so intoxicating, and so radical you only have to get the tiniest taste of Him to want more.

I invited my friend Lizzy to Jesus Burgers a few times. Although hesitant at first, she finally decided to come one night. I remember telling her, "Okay, but I'm warning you, it might change your life!"

The night that Lizzy attended Jesus Burgers, she accepted Jesus Christ into her life as her Lord and Savior. The next morning she came to my house and had the hugest smile on her face. "Dude! You were right! It changed my life!!!"

I am witnessing every day how God is moving in this city. He is bringing hope, joy, and revival here. He is showing Himself to a generation that is looking for love, just as I was. Let me tell you, I've finally found it.

SHED
LIFE

RYAN ELLIS

A s I sit here in a coffee shop, trying to find the words to encapsulate every detail that has brought me to where I am today, I find myself teary eyed and speechless. It feels almost impossible for me to give this story the magnitude it deserves, because it is ultimately God's story. He deserves so much glory with His perfect timing and His way of intricately weaving divine appointments, encounters, and situations. We have a faithful Father. He never gives up, never stops loving, never stops pursuing us and who He made us to be. HE WILL NEVER GIVE UP ON US! My story is one of the victories of the consistent pursuit of God's love. He's been after me since the beginning.

I grew up in the beautiful city of San Diego, California. I was given a lot of responsibility at a very young age. My mom worked long hours and her boyfriends would come and go. I was usually left at home watching my little brother, so I had to grow up fast. I felt like I was raising myself. With no father figure and no respect for authority, I quickly got into a lot of trouble.

135

At the age of fourteen I started breaking into houses and doing drugs. My neighbor was a drug supplier, so I started selling drugs as well. Eventually, my ghetto life caught up with me, and I was arrested for selling drugs. I was kicked out of the San Diego School District. I auditioned to get into a performing arts school, and the director took a chance on me and let me in.

You could say I sang and danced my way out of the judicial system. I became involved with some of the most prestigious performing arts programs in San Diego. I was part of elite dance teams such as Future Shock SD, Formality, and Jabbawockeez, on top of musical theater and earning scholarships for ballet. Amidst this success, I was surrounded by some older men who knew Christ and began planting seeds that God was faithful to water.

I joined the United States Navy after graduating high school. There I continued self-destructive patterns of engulfing myself in alcohol, drugs, and sex. I began to spiral down into a deep depression. Once I enlisted, I didn't speak with my mother for two years. Then she started sending me text messages of Bible verses, which only frustrated me, or maybe just convicted me. She called me one day and began to tell me about how she accepted Jesus and that God had been putting me on her heart. I broke down crying. I finally saw how lost I was and that only God could get me out of the mess I had created. It was then that I accepted Jesus, but that was just the beginning. I had no idea how much the Father actually loved me or even liked me.

After accepting Christ and still being in the Navy, I was sent to Afghanistan. There I looked for suicide bombers and roadside bombs, and I did construction on base. After a year of being overseas, I returned with such a hard heart towards God because of the lack of value for life I had experienced. Guilt and shame covered my heart as I thought about the questions that I felt could never be answered. I became angry at the church because I felt like no one understood what I had just gone through. People would casually ask, "How many people did you kill?" and "Did you ever see anyone get blown up?" Feeling condemned and misunderstood pushed me further and further away from the church. I became isolated in my shame and went back to my old ways.

When you know the Truth, going back to a life that is not who you were created to be is unbearable. For a year I battled with the anger. My family was in constant prayer, and God answered those prayers. One night I finally broke down and cried out, "God, I'm so tired of being angry and not knowing why!" He came in like a flood and washed away anger, shame, and guilt. I felt His peace overcome me as a year of confusion, questions, and frustrations came out. He took it all away and made me new. Jesus met me where I was, Hallelujah! After that night I was on fire for the Lord. I was baptized in the Holy Spirit and started seeing the Father show up in the most amazing ways.

I was living in Ventura when God started bringing me to Isla Vista through some amazing divine appointments. It started by God calling me to drive to UCSB. I would walk around campus just getting lost and wondering why I was there. Since I never attended college, I thought maybe God was saying that I would be going to UCSB, but nope! It was the people on campus whom He was slowly putting on my heart.

One night a friend brought me up to Isla Vista to visit his friend who lived in a house where they hand out hamburgers to the city on Friday nights. When I arrived at the Jesus Burgers house, I was not prepared for what I saw. We had a time of worship and prayer, then we went out to the front of the house to see thousands of students walking up and down Del Playa Drive looking for the craziest party. There are many different reactions to the party scene in IV. Some get angry, confused, or offended, but my heart was excited. I was able to see that the harvest was plentiful, and I knew God was going to do epic things there.

I saw a group of guys standing in front of me and walked up to them. I said, "Hey bro, you have some pain in your shoulder?" He looked at me and said, "Nope." Then I looked at his friend and said, "God wants to put joy in your heart because you've been angry for a long time." All of his friends started laughing at him because they call him "The Grinch." The first guy I spoke to asked, "How did you know about my shoulder?" I just smiled and said to him, "It's your right one, and because God is real and He loves you!" They all started to freak out. I proceeded to prophesy over each of them, and they ran around the street yelling, "Jesus is real, this dude is telling me everything about me and my family!" Then we prayed over his shoulder, and it was healed. The group of guys wanted to get baptized, so we went down to the ocean and baptized them. It was an awesome night.

After a couple of visits to Isla Vista, I led worship with Mac Montgomery on Halloween. The presence of God was heavy in the prayer house. Being the amazing visionary that Mac is, the next morning he spoke to me and said that he saw me leading worship in Isla Vista and being a part of what God was doing in this city. Feeling like my ministry was in Ventura, I was hesitant to move to IV. I talked with Jason Lomelino, who said the same thing as Mac. I've always been a person who is 100 percent committed to whatever I am doing. I've surrendered my whole life to God and want to be sold out for His will. I want to be led wherever the Holy Spirit leads me. Saying yes to Jesus is so exciting, and I didn't want to pass up something He was doing. I prayed, then called my good friend Matt. He answered the phone and said, "Wait, before you say anything, I was praying and God said that you are moving to Isla Vista." I proceeded to freak out in my car and took it as confirmation.

The next week I got a text from Jason asking if I could build him a shed. I was surprised at such a random question, but I said yes. He then explained that he wanted me to build a shed on his property and that God told him that I should live in the shed for six months to be closely discipled by him and get to know his family. I felt God's peace over it, even though it sounded bananas. I told him yes. That was the beginning of my "Shed Life." It was the hardest season of my life. It was the goodness of the Father and His sweet discipline to lead me into a transformation season where I was completely naked with God and surrounded by total strangers.

I experienced the true love and grace of God through this family and community. No matter how much I kicked, screamed, cried, felt misunderstood, got homesick, or even was content and flourishing, this family loved me. They continued to speak truth to me, saw my identity when I couldn't, and picked me up and carried me when I couldn't walk. I have never experienced that type of love or church family. The Father completely ripped my heart open, did heart surgery, and unveiled my identity as a son. I learned that my life was already a success in God's eyes because there's nothing I can do to change His love for me and how He sees me. I learned that my value wasn't based on performance or what I did for

God, and I learned how to dwell in the secret place and have daily intimacy with Him.

I am forever grateful for Jason, Mac, Eric, and many others who fought for me when I did not want to fight. Though the shed life was hard, I wouldn't trade that season of my life for anything in this world. Matthew 10:39 says, "He who finds his life will lose it, and he who loses his life for My sake will find it." God is so much more concerned with our hearts than what we can do for Him. Our identity rests in being sons and daughters of the Sovereign King Jesus, Creator of All, the Great I AM, the Alpha and the Omega, and LOVE Himself! If you're not operating in that reality, then you are open game for the enemy to have a field day and tear you down with guilt, shame, and condemnation. But hey, we are the ones who are here to stomp out hell for a living and release the Kingdom of Heaven!

I currently build up saints for battle in the Jesus Burgers house on Del Playa, just as I was built up. I love releasing people into their identity and introducing them to their Father who loves them. I will be here in Isla Vista until I am called somewhere else, and I will continue daily to destroy the works of the enemy with love as my weapon. God is doing amazing things here, and I am honored to be a part of Heaven's history, even if it meant living in a shed for a while.

HE RESTORED
MY HEART

CALEB DAVIS

There once was a boy named Caleb. He grew up secure in God's love. He had dreams about Jesus and angels from the time he was a small child. He loved God and was fully aware of Heaven and His expanding Kingdom on the earth. He knew who he was. His identity was in Jesus. Caleb had made his home in Him. His relationship to Jesus was the most important relationship in his life.

This was my story until I was about nine-years-old and my parents got divorced. The circumstances were beyond my understanding, but it shook my foundation to rubble, and I no longer knew what to believe anymore. I knew my parents still loved me, but why didn't they love each other anymore? Why couldn't they work this problem out? Where was God? How could He let this happen? With all these questions, my identity was quickly lost, and I wouldn't find it again for ten years. Those ten years were full of loneliness, anxiety, fear, depression, and self-destructive behaviors to cope with all those negative aspects of my life. I looked for love in all the wrong places—in friends, in girls, in drugs, and in alcohol—but my strongest addiction was music. I loved music, and before I met Jesus again, music was a huge idol in my life. I now realize music has been so important to me because of a call to be a worship leader. Music has always been the fastest and easiest way for me to connect with God. Satan had perverted my true passion and calling of musical worship into an unhealthy idolization of music, but God restored this passion and this calling to its full realization.

Through all the sex, drugs, and rock and roll, I made it out alive, but my heart had become cold and hard, bearing all the scars of those dark years. At this point, I was nineteen-years-old, living on the street, and feeling completely abandoned by God. One night I had been drinking heavily, as I usually did, then I took a handful of pills from someone at a party, hoping the pills would knock me out or kill me. When the pills, which were apparently uppers, made me wide awake and even more frustrated with life, I decided to go on a walk to get them out of my system faster. I walked for hours until I ended up on State Street in downtown Santa Barbara. It was around four in the morning; all the bars had closed and nobody was out. I sat on a ledge outside a bar and stared at the street, trying to take my focus off of my life and how it had spiraled out of control.

Then God stepped in.

A man walked up to me drinking what he said was gin out of a Mountain Dew bottle. There was something different about him, but the lack of sleep and intoxication had kept me from paying too much attention to it. He offered me a sip of his bottle, and I accepted. Anything to drown out the pain. He asked me why I was out here. I told him what was going on in my life and that the real reason I was out here was because I couldn't get along with my father. He looked straight into my eyes and said in a serious but warm tone, "You need to call your father." I told him I didn't have a phone and didn't want to call him. He said he had a phone and insisted that I call my dad right away. It was now about six in the morning, and I could hear birds chirping through the fog. I called my dad and he picked up. The man gave me the words to say to him because I knew I couldn't say them on my own. I repeated after him saying, "Dad, I need you. I need you to help me." My dad came and picked me up, but not before the man had me write his cell phone number on my arm with a pen so I could call him later and let him know I had made it home safely. My dad picked me up downtown, and we didn't exchange one word the whole ride back to his house. Little did we know that this was the beginning of my redemption, my return home, and restoration of my rightful place and identity. After I woke up the next day, I called the number and was surprised to find an automated voice message say that it was not an actual phone number. I had just called my dad from that number the night before, and the number was on my dad's phone log still! I now believe that man was an angel. The more I thought about it, the more I realized God was working in my life. He had not abandoned me. This messenger of God didn't come to condemn my lifestyle or scare me into repentance. He came with kindness and met me where I was. He pointed me to my Father, both earthly and heavenly.

After about a year of reading only my Bible, helping out at a local church's Youth Group, and praying everyday to relearn how to live with God, Jesus had once again become the most important relationship in my life. My identity had been restored.

The second most important relationship in my life began in 2009, when I met the girl who would later become my wife. Haley has always been the most real example of Jesus to me. I remember reading the Gospels and Jesus telling His disciples to "believe!" and "have faith!" One time while on a walk with Haley, I had been sharing different doubts and fears that I had in my life. After I had gotten it all out, she turned to me and responded gently by saying, "Caleb, you need to have more faith." In ways like this and with her unchanging, unconditional love for me, she helped me grow more and more back into that identity I had lost when my parents divorced.

Life went on. Haley and I were growing in God and more and more in love with each other, but we had always felt a disconnect at the churches we attended. There were few people our age, and few who shared in our passions. There was more restoration that God wanted to bring us into. We began praying diligently for God to provide us with a community, friends who would live life alongside us. During this time, my brother had begun helping out at Jesus Burgers and always invited me to come check it out. This family that gave burgers out once a week was what Haley and I had been praying for all along.

One Sunday afternoon, I was riding my bike through Isla Vista and saw a group of college kids standing in front of a house. I realized after reading a sign in front that it was the Isla Vista Church congregating at Pastor Jason's house. ("These are the Jesus Burgers people," I thought to myself.) I got off my bike and was greeted by Ian, a friendly college student with dreadlocks. He invited me in. The second I set foot on the property, I was drenched in the love of God. I had never felt God's love in such a real, tangible way before. I couldn't explain it, but I couldn't deny it. I walked around to the back of the house and sat down in one of the chairs, while a small worship team tuned up their instruments before the service started. The worship leader began singing. The second the words came out, I could feel the Holy Spirit begin to fall and rest upon us—weaving between everyone there, wrapping them in love, renewing strength, releasing joy, and bestowing peace upon everyone present. I worshipped more freely and more openly than I had in years, and to songs that I had never even heard before! The worship leader sang a line that said, "I'm running through your fields of freedom, and the castle of religion is far behind." I had never heard such beautiful worship or such powerful words. I knew this was the place God wanted Haley and I. Later that day, I told Haley about Isla Vista Church and how "God's love was so real there that you could reach out and touch it." Soon enough we both started attending all of the church's events regularly, including Jesus Burgers.

One of my fondest memories of Jesus Burgers was in the summer of 2013. It was on this night that I re-learned a great lesson: working with God is easy, and all it requires is a little bit of faith. From the get go, it seemed that this night was going to be pretty laid-back and uneventful. Many students had gone home for summer vacation, and even the attendance for our Upper Room service that takes place before Jesus Burgers was smaller than usual. I had been in a pretty dry spot spiritually and was not expecting anything miraculous to happen that night. With what little faith I had for the night, I went out from the Upper Room service ready to work with Jesus that night and whatever He had planned for me.

As the night progressed, I noticed something different about the few people coming in to get burgers. They all had beautiful Irish accents! The Irish students who came to work and party in Isla Vista during the summer came in full force that night. While standing in the kitchen of the Jesus Burgers house, I was approached by a girl from the ministry asking if I wanted to help them pray for someone. I said sure, not expecting to do anything on this night besides watch other people evangelize. The boy who they were praying for introduced himself as Stephen and shook my hand. After shaking my hand, he quickly raised it to cover his eye. It seemed to be irritating him, and I quickly found out that I had been asked to come over to help pray for his eye. He had gotten something in it, and it was extremely swollen and irritated. He couldn't see out of it and had just tried washing it out in the sink. There were about three or four of us gathered around Stephen to pray for his eye. We asked permission one more time just to be sure that he was okay with us praying for it. He agreed and was more than happy to receive some prayer as nothing else had seemed to work.

I placed my hand gently on his eye and vocally welcomed the Holy Spirit to come and restore his eye. I felt the presence of God rest on my head and travel the length of my arm and onto Stephen. I asked if the pain was any better or if he felt anything. While still holding his beer in the other hand, Stephen began nodding and smiling, saying, "Yes, it feels better, keep praying." We continued praying for healing and full restoration of his eye. Soon it was completely back to normal. Stephen was jumping up and down, shouting, "Jesus!" and fist pumping with the hand that had been covering his eye. It was a humorous sight, that gave those of us who had prayed for him so much joy.

God had healed with just the little faith I had to contribute that night. But my favorite part of this story was what God had done to Stephen's heart. After we celebrated and hugged for a little bit, Stephen began to share with us his entire religious history. Having been raised in the Catholic Church in Ireland, he told us he had "spent all of his life learning about God and Jesus" in private school and in church. But it had all been "a lot of words" about God and His Son. It had never been more than superstition and religion. But that night he told us he had finally "seen the Power of God" and that "Jesus is real!" For the rest of the night Stephen went to every one of his friends and told them about how God is real and that He heals. It was a beautiful thing to see this Irish kid's heart suddenly burn with zeal for God from a simple act of faith on our part. And it was humbling to see God work a miracle even when I wasn't expecting anything to happen.

Since becoming a part of Isla Vista Church and moving into community there, I have seen God heal people from many different physical ailments. More importantly, I have seen God heal the hearts of His children. God is in the business of full restoration — body, mind, soul, spirit, and heart. Jesus was sent to "bind up the brokenhearted." Now that Jesus lives in us, we are anointed to bring comfort to the brokenhearted just as He does. The King is here, He has restored us, and we are free to love as He does, holding nothing back! Now that I have been restored, I am able to help restore others who are lost like I was. My story is a simple one. God restored my broken heart so that I could love others the way He does.

HE MADE
A PLACE
FOR ME

HANNAH VIDMAR

God is perfect in all His ways. God loves to invade our lives and set aside a place for us to freely receive His love and affection. He created a place for me in His Kingdom. By bringing me to the Jesus Burgers house, He made a place for me in everyday life on this earth. He has a place for everyone. He invites all to take their place and join in the song that gives Him glory.

I grew up overseas in a place called Almaty, Kazakhstan, because my parents felt called by God to live there. It was my home from the time I was eight till I was sixteen, when I returned to northern California, where I finished my last two years of school. The transition back to the States was difficult since I realized that I did not have a home on this earth. I understood that I would always be longing for my heavenly home. I grew up in a home exposed to different churches and ministries, which also included people who were burnt out with ministry, church, and, eventually, God. I had a huge fear in my life that I would become one of these burnt-out Christians or stop following God. God was always a part of my life,

149

but the past few years I've truly fallen in love with Him and found out what a relationship with Him really looks like.

I applied to universities while attending high school, but none accepted me. This rejection was difficult for me because I put much of my worth in how well I performed. I told myself it was all right to not go to college, because I wanted to get out of America. In my attempt to escape, I attended a Discipleship Training School with YWAM in Australia. It was the only door I felt God left open. While there, I really encountered God's love for me and received the revelation that the majestic Creator of the universe had a fierce love for me. The feeling that His eyes are forever fixed on me and in love with me will never get old and will remain the foundation of my relationship with Him.

I returned to my little hometown in northern California and attended community college without having much direction in life, but still with having a desire to attend a university. Through that time, I really fell in love with God. While no one was looking, I tried to find Him even in the places I thought were dry and boring. During this season, I was invited to a Jesus Culture conference at the last minute. I encountered His presence as I just cried and cried. I didn't know why I was crying, and I didn't know why I couldn't stop. I was actually really mad that I was crying, because I felt like I couldn't worship God. It's funny because now I know that was the truest worship I could have had, and He would not have wanted me raising my hands, singing, dancing, or performing in any way for Him. He wanted to stop me from pursuing Him all the time so He could fiercely pursue me.

The following year, I watched the Jesus Culture conference online and turned it on during a segment about seeing the Kingdom of God invade college and high school campuses. A student from UCSB, Cassie, talked about her experience with Jesus Burgers. I knew there was something different about her. I felt she was part of a community and family doing something in the heart of God with an authenticity that I found hard to come across in the Western church. I had already applied to UC Santa Barbara and thought to myself, "If I get into UCSB, I am totally checking that place out!" Months later, UCSB accepted me as a global studies major. I had found out thirty minutes before my baptism at a friend's house. There was a rainbow in the sky that evening, a little gift to show me that God does not go back on His promises and the desires He has placed in my heart.

When I decided to attend UCSB, I somehow missed out on my housing application. I was a little anxious, but also felt that I was not supposed to live on campus-supplied housing. I tried not to worry; but as the summer approached, I still didn't have a place. I didn't even know anyone who went to UCSB or lived in Isla Vista. One day, I randomly found out Jesus Burgers was a part of a church, so I looked up Isla Vista Church and found a post from a couple of weeks prior that said, "One more spot for a lady at the Jesus Burgers house, heaven knows who this lady is, yay God!" I read that and started to cry, but still did not have the faith to believe, "Oh that's going to be my home." I kept thinking, "No way, this couldn't be God. Does He even care about where I would live? Would He really hand pick a place for me?" Usually students in Isla Vista know where they are going to live by January, and this was already late July. After contacting the church, Jason called me and told me how one of the girls from the Jesus Burgers house was not returning to Santa Barbara. The next weekend, I drove down to visit the church and see the house. I attended the church service in the Lomelinos' backyard, and the first song was called "He Made a Place For Me." Two weeks later I was moving into the Jesus Burgers house, about to begin the best year of my life.

It was incredible to be immersed in a community that was so focused and obedient to Jesus and carried the simplicity of loving Him and loving others. I would get so excited because I had never seen a community love God like this. It felt to me like all of Heaven's attention was on IV, preparing for things beyond any of our imaginations. I was passionate about seeing revival invade my city and college campus, but Jesus was also concerned about my identity and my heart. He is good and perfect in all His ways. He makes sure our hearts host true and sustainable revival first so that a college campus, city, or nation can be blessed through it. It was life changing to be in a place with such good soil, where I could grow and learn without trying to fight against anything by myself. I was able to experience the acceleration and the freedom that community gave me to find out more of who I am in Jesus.

I was just someone trying to find a place to live, and behind the scenes God was planning so much more. It was such an eye opener in my life to see that God is actually real in my life and cares about every detail, even the place I live. He created a place better than I could have even imagined. People try so hard to create a community or a life that they want. When we give up and let God do it, it works out a lot better, and we end up getting so much more than we could ever even ask for.

I believe that He will give Isla Vista and so many people what He promised for their college campus and their own lives. I can see how the world watches and is influenced by the culture of the U.S., specifically California. If people from so many nations watch California, then how incredible it would be if they could see the Kingdom and meet King Jesus. For so long I had wanted to leave the States and move somewhere else, somewhere I felt people were hungry and God was moving in crazy ways. But God can't be limited. I have seen more healings and more moves of God in the States now than I have anywhere else. People are hungry everywhere, and Jesus is the desire of everyone's heart—whether they know it yet or not.

Every Friday night at Jesus Burgers, we talk, encourage, or pray with different people. A lot of the time, we never know if it had any impact on their life. But one thing I have realized: no matter how much time or effort I put into a ministry, Jesus returns it with overflowing life. Doing Jesus Burgers has shown me that it is not the work of ministry that bears the best fruit, but it is life in the Kingdom. This life does not beat us to the ground and burn us out, but is how we are naturally supposed to live.

I love how much Jesus emphasizes being a good neighbor and representation of Him. During Deltopia, an all day and night weekend party in IV, one of my favorite memories was of multiple people in a row coming up and wanting to hang out with us. They told us that they found us more accepting and welcoming than the other houses where they were trying to party. I personally felt so blessed by this, because in my life I usually encounter people who are bitter against the church and have had horrible examples from the church of what Jesus looks like. They were blown away with how accepted they felt, and I know it is supposed to be like this with every person who encounters a believer. They should feel the most loved, the most accepted, and the least judged, because this is what Jesus does as He invites us into His home. Now we can spend the rest of our lives inviting everyone else into the perfect place He has made for them!

I know now that my fear of burnout and leaving God is irrational, because it was never my job to sustain our relationship in the first place. He did it all, and He will continue to do the rest. This does not mean that I will stop seeking and loving Him; it just means I will trust in the perfect God and not fear. He showed me that His perfect love casts out all fear and that He will not let go of me. Jesus has recently shown me the sweet truth that He is my home. This seems too good to be true, especially for someone who knows what it feels like to miss or lack a home. I no longer have to be miserable on earth waiting for my heavenly home, because now I know that no matter where I am, I can feel at home in Him. He has made a place for me here in Isla Vista, and He has made a home for me in His heart. Now I can feel permanently at home with Him forever.

God Is
Better

BRYCE SOLTES

I once learned in a Psychology of Memory class that we humans tend to remember the most emotional events from our past. It makes sense then why I vividly remember at age four telling my grandma that I asked Jesus into my heart; that moment has marked me forever. I now live at the Jesus Burgers house, helping to oversee the night, so apparently that four-year-old's prayer worked.

Perhaps you can already tell I grew up in the church; however, I hated it. For years I would beg and scream for my parents not to take me. I had a hard time making friends at church, and I didn't care about the teachings. So from childhood through adolescence, while I claimed to be a Christian, I was very apathetic towards anything related to God. My biggest care was how people saw me, which led to an obsession with being popular in high school. I was consumed with others' opinions of me, so I bought all the "right" clothes and tried to hang out with the "right" people because I was too afraid to act like myself. The crippling fear of looking dumb in front of the popular kids kept my mouth shut and actually got me excluded from all the parties. But even despite that, I thought nothing could be better than popularity, so that's what I pursued.

In my sophomore year of high school, something clicked, and I decided to ask Jesus into my heart again. I have no idea what prompted it (probably the Holy Spirit), but sitting on my couch, I invited Jesus in. Immediately, this indescribable warmth and peace came over me. I couldn't stop smiling and had no idea what was happening! I still did not understand who Jesus was or who I was, but this instance felt good, and I liked it. I started going to church more and even attending our high school Christian club. But there still wasn't any real change in my life. I had several addictions, and all I cared about was being popular, going to college, and getting a girlfriend. By the end of high school, I stuck around my local church long enough to get me some good church friends. I even got a girlfriend and got accepted into a good college! Life seemed to be getting better. That is, until I watched my dad have a seizure.

Seeing my dad so helpless was one of the worst things I have seen in my life, and another moment I am not likely to forget. After he had a few seizures, he was given tests, but nothing came up outside of a dot on his brain that was too small to affect anything. Though frightened, I distracted myself with my new journey of attending UC Santa Barbara. Once I arrived, I wanted friends and that ever-elusive popularity. I didn't want "bad" friends, so I joined the local Campus Crusade for Christ. It was great. I became instantly connected to a great community of believers who were in love with God and wanted others to know Him. People cared enough about me to encourage my personal and spiritual growth and rally around me in times of need, which were about to come.

During winter quarter of my freshmen year in college, my dad visited me. He took me to dinner one night and told me the doctors found out what that dot in his head was. I remember the breathlessness I felt as my father—the one who made me laugh so much as a child, the one I could nerd out with about Star Wars and super heroes, my hero growing up— told me that he had stage four brain cancer and two years to live. I didn't know what to do. All I knew was that I needed God. When he dropped me off at my dorm room, I immediately went inside, broke down, grabbed my Bible, and tearfully begged my room- mate, "Don't let me lose my faith." I had a choice to make those next few years: Was I going to blame God for this? Or, knowing He is better than death, was I going to cling to Him? By His mercy and grace, I chose the latter.

The next two years were full of suffering, growth, and love. I am eternally grateful for the community I had around me; they mourned with me, spent time with me, and directed me to Jesus at all times. If it weren't for my house being built on the rock, when this storm hit, I would have crumbled. My dad's health began to deteriorate as I grew in knowing the Lord. For the first year or so, my dad seemed the same, may- be forgetting a word here and there.

One of my favorite memories is from my soph- omore year, when we were baptized together. That same year, I also started attending Isla Vista Church. I was so curious about these crazy Jesus-loving people who were incredibly genuine and had the craziest stories about life with God. I met the pastor, Jason, and would meet up with him throughout the year. That was a relationship that I have valued tremen- dously over the years.

Eventually, my dad's health started getting worse.

I remember seeing him after he had a seizure during a surgery; he was hooked up to a breathing tube and all sorts of wires, completely unconscious. As soon as I saw him, I couldn't talk and started feeling sick. I went to the bathroom and began talking to God. He encouraged me in that time, giving me reasons to not fear or dismay. Cancer has been defeated. Death has been defeated. This life is only temporary, and nothing can separate us from His love; nothing can compare to Him. The entire world looks ahead to death, unless they know their Creator. God is better than this world, and I know Him. I left that bathroom still saddened, but with a newfound joy and peace. Driving home a day later, the doctor called and told us it was normal for someone to have a seizure during that surgery, which comforted us.

Later on, my dad's speech was reduced to mumbles, he could barely see, and he was confined to a wheelchair. We moved him to a hospice, and many times I left that place in tears seeing him in such a state. Every time, my God would speak to me and show me how much better He is than this world, and that this is not the end. My most cherished memory of my dad during this time was when he gave me a call while I was away at school. I could understand next to nothing of what he was saying, but the one thing I was able to make out was, "I love you." My father loved me, and that was all I needed to hear.

It was on December 20, 2011, that my dad went to be with Jesus. It was a year before that to the day, even to the hour, that we were baptized together on December 20, 2010. God knew what was happening, as He is the master of life and death. Blessed are those who mourn, for they will be comforted. I have mourned, and I have been comforted.

The next few years, I grew in my love for God,

trusting and believing that He is the greatest there is. Nothing can compare to Him, for we were created for Him. How can we live for anything less than what we were created for? I had my own struggles, but God was faithful to deliver me and lovingly teach me that His way is the best, most joyful, peaceful, and loving way. I learned so much from the genuine love from my family in Campus Crusade and in Isla Vista Church. God taught me and loved me so well during those next few years, revealing Himself as a Father like never before.

He teaches you, lifts you up, embraces you, and will never reject you if you turn to Him. His love for us is so pure that nothing we can do will cause His opinion of us to change. All of this is because while we were still sinners, Christ died for us (Romans 5:8). It is all because of Jesus! In Hebrews 2:10, it says of Jesus, "for whom and by whom all things exist." Everything is for Him! If everything is for Him, how could He not turn something as horrible as death into something good?

Death is terrible, cancer is terrible, but praise God that all things work for good for those who love Him (Romans 8). I have come in contact with countless people who have either lost their father, never met their father, or have a father who is currently terminally ill. I have been able to minister to and counsel most, if not all, of these people I have met who have some type of parent issue. By experiencing the suffering I have, I can relate to, and open doors for, conversations and encounters with God that maybe would not have happened otherwise. Some may say the vast amount of people I have met who deal with these issues have been all coincidences, but I disagree. After following God for a few years and seeing and hearing enough crazy stories firsthand, I have come to the conclusion that I do not believe in coincidences anymore. I have seen many of these stories come to pass at Jesus Burgers, where the harvest is plentiful!

I was first connected with Jesus Burgers through my attendance at the local Campus Crusade for Christ. I had friends who would go out regularly to pass out burgers to partiers and talk to them about Jesus. However, I did not participate nearly as much as some of my friends. Immaturity and fear gripped me, causing me to shy away from talking to others about Jesus. Eventually, I started attending Isla Vista Church, where I met amazing, genuine people. Something about their love and joy attracted me, so I stuck around, plus the free food was nice. I was still fairly immature and was not very involved in the church for a few years. Thank God that He matures us so fast! By my senior year in college, much of the fear I had three years prior was waning, being replaced with love. This new courage allowed me to speak passionately about Jesus to those who were willing to hear. The passion I had drew me to overseas missions in the Middle East for a year, where I told hundreds about Jesus. Once I came back to America, I was ready to go all in for ministry, and I felt God leading me back to my college town of Santa Barbara to continue and deepen my involvement in Isla Vista Church. I would often stay up late into the night on the Jesus Burgers nights talking to the stragglers long after the burgers were gone. The time spent on Fridays has now led me to live in the ministry house where we give out the burgers. There is so much opportunity for ministry to partiers, homeless, Christians, and anyone else who comes near our house, and I love it!

However, the Friday night outreach is definitely the most defining aspect of the house. I remember one particular night at Jesus Burgers that I went out evangelizing. I took a group out on the streets to talk to people and pray for them in the craziness of a Friday night. We stood across the street from a group of intimidating-looking guys, and I felt God tell me that one in particular never knew his father. I was hesitant to ask, but there is something about Jesus Burgers, and well, Jesus, that gives you boldness you do not normally have.

I walked up to the guy and tried to diffuse the awkwardness of the question as best as I could. "Was your dad around for you when you were young?" I asked. That is something I never would have even thought about doing when I was consumed with people's opinions of me in high school.

He responded by telling me he had actually never met his father. I was able to pray with him and declare the Father's love over him right there. Afterwards, he told me most of what I said was true and what he was currently experiencing. As soon as he revealed that to me, his friend pulled him away to continue down the street, as so often happens when we talk to people. I have no idea what happened to that guy, but he knew that there was a God who legitimately cared about him, and he knew what to do if he should want to know his true Father.

There have been other stories like that one. I've seen conversations instantly change and hearts open up once a person hears how my dad died, because that person's dad currently has cancer too. What started out as a surface-level conversation becomes an opportunity for the Father to lavish His child with love and comfort. God has even spoken to me directly about a guy whose father abandoned his family when he was three-years-old.

I've met so many different people who are comforted by how God brought me through this journey with my dad and how He spoke to me throughout it.

And in every conversation, I share the story about how God is better than what this world offers.

Jesus Burgers has been the perfect environment to meet people who are in desperate need of their Father in Heaven. Some are looking for an escape from their problems, some are looking for an experience, some are looking to feel better about themselves, but all are looking for life. Jesus promises life and life abundantly. That's why we are outside every Friday night. We are there to tell people that everything they want and need is found in Jesus, and that He is better.

JUST A
DAUGHTER

BRITTANY CARRIGER

I've always been involved with spirituality on some level. In my formative years, I was raised by three primary care-givers other than my mother: Grandmama, a Baptist; Grandmere, a Seventh Day Adventist; and Aunt Najama, a Muslim.

I was very young, so my concept of each religion was very narrow, but I do remember that I had three sets of rules to follow and one "Gnarly Dude in the Sky" who would send me to hell if I missed one answer on the big quiz at the end of time.

My parents were very young and pretty focused on their music. They believed in God, and Jesus was definitely a good guy too, but music was more important. With that came drugs for my dad, and my mom, at age twenty-four, spent all of her spare time caring for her drug-addicted husband and two children under the age of three. Life was what it was for a while, until I turned five—and everything changed.

One would think that those short five years couldn't have been more of a trip, but alas that would be wrong. My father's drug use caught up to him. He overdosed at thirty-six-years-old, three months before my kindergarten graduation.

A month later, his mama, Grandmama, died of heartbreak. A year after that, Grandmere died of breast cancer. A few short months after that, Aunt Najama died of lung cancer. Having faced four close, painful deaths after seven years in the world, it was easy to feel abandoned. When a lot of people die at once, the inevitability of death and the afterlife becomes more of a reality. And that God dude seems a lot scarier. I really wanted to make sure that I didn't make him mad. Any involvement I had with church was multiplied, exponentially.

My parents were incredible musicians, and I inherited some of their abilities. I noticed that when I sang at church, people would not just like me, they would love me. They noticed me and filled my craving to be loved. Thus, I figured out early on that the more I sang, the more friends I would have. I was a sharp kid; being faced with the inevitability of your own death at seven-years-old will do that to you. I could ask questions that would even baffle the Bible study teachers. At ten-years-old, I voluntarily enrolled in the fast track class to baptism and was baptized in the Seventh Day Adventist church.

As a great church-goer and quite popular with the adults, you would think I would have a million friends, right? Well, not really. My mom moved all of the time, for a lot of reasons. Money, men, money . . . and then men. This moving meant changing schools, a lot. I was always a lonely kid. When my mom got tired of the church, I lost that too.

At age twelve, we moved next door to this pastor dude. He was pretty nice to us, and after my mom had gone from musician to actor, etc., she decided to marry the pastor dude. It seemed like the safest place for everyone, and we were back in church. But this was different. It was a storefront Pentecostal church, definitely not my jam in any way, shape, or form. This was my only chance of having a dad, so I was going to do my best to make him like me. I did the only things I knew to do to make adults like me: I started studying my Bible, really hard, and I sang in his church. Everyone loved me! But the thing is, pastor dude didn't really seem to notice at all. He wasn't very nice to me or to our family.

Someone did notice me. Someone above was watching me really closely. At twelve, I was baptized in the Holy Spirit. It was the most intense experience I'd ever had. I was speaking a language I didn't know (also known as tongues) and felt God's presence all over me. Apparently, God actually wanted to come live inside of me. It was better than any feeling in the world. Nonetheless, pastor dude still didn't like me, and other than my church friends, I didn't have friends at school. They called me Jesus' baby. It was way hard to find a date to prom.

When I went to UCSB as a theater major, first thing I did was search for a church to get that love again. I joined a number of groups and worshiped with two major ones on campus. I knew nearly every Christian on campus, but I was still a lonely, sad kid. It felt like no matter what I did, I got lonelier. On top of that, I would end up in the wrong relationships and not nurture the ones that mattered.

Even though I tried to make friends with believers, the partiers just seemed a little bit cooler. I was drawn to the party life of UCSB and the freedom I hadn't known from the sheltered Islamic/Adventist/Baptist/Pentecostal homes. At home, the white man, hip hop music, and pork were all the devil. But here in Isla Vista, white people were super friendly, hip hop music was fun to dance to, and pork was delicious!

So I began to live a "secret" life. The Christian people would get a good little girl, Monday through Thursday. But I would sneak out as soon as I could to play with the cool party kids in IV.

When I wasn't partying, I met the Jesus Burgers people through one of the many church groups I was involved with. It was different. In all my striving to make this mean God happy (joining worship teams, doing service, etc.), I had found this place where there was no need to strive. Because no matter who you were or where you came from, you were loved, and there was nothing you could do about it. Jesus Burgers was better than anything I had ever known, and the associated church, IVC, was really cool too. I even spent the majority of a summer trying to understand this new God who was nice and loving.

Although I was spending time with these Jesus people, I was afraid that it was all too good to be true. I feared that they would either reject me like my pastor dad dude or die on me like everyone else. When fall came, I separated myself from them, and the growth that I was achieving with these Jesus Burgers people halted. But I loved Jesus, and I knew He loved me. I didn't know how deep that love went until much later.

I tried really hard to be okay with the life I was living. By the world's standards. I was successful. I was a college-educated black woman and a well-read individual. My lifestyle, by the world's standards, was nowhere near wild. I never rushed into relationships. I was rarely drunk. I had never blacked out. I lost my virtue at twenty-one in a consenting, open, and communicative relationship. So why did I feel so dark and empty? Why did I hate myself so much? Why was I in so much pain?

The night that I ended that consenting, open, and communicative relationship was when the floor collapsed beneath me. The young man and I decided to end amicably, with ideological differences stated as the cause. I was still a Christian, albeit lukewarm, and he was not . . . so it just wouldn't work. Still, I wanted him deep down in my heart.

With the relationship over, I was broken. I gave him the most precious part of me, and he was supposed to love me for it. It felt like my whole world was turned upside down. I felt like my whole entire soul was ripped out of my heart. I hopped on my bike, my heart beating into my ears. I roamed from house to house, sobbing, looking for some kind of confirmation, some hope that I would survive, some comfort. I landed at a friend's house, who was not a Christian, but "enlightened," and he looked at me without pity and said, with ice in his voice: "Brittany, you did this to yourself."

Unable to think or breathe, I got on my bike and rode as hard and fast as I could. At one o'clock in the morning I found myself scuttling up the Jesus Burgers stairs and pounding on the door. My friend Tenaya lived there, and she had known about the situation; surely, she would have something to say. She opened the door, and when I looked into her eyes, I saw something that melted all of my pride, fear of rejection, and self-hatred. It was the love of Jesus. She held open her arms, and they became the arms of the Father. I said nothing and collapsed into her arms, wailing and gasping. All I could manage through the tears were two phrases: "Everything hurts," and "I feel like I'm dying."

Without question or hesitation, every girl who lived in that house, all seven, got out of their beds in their pajamas with blankets and pillows, made a bed for me, laid hands on me, and prayed for me. At that moment, the love of Jesus was demonstrated in such a profound way. That moment changed everything for me. That moment stuck with me.

Out of college, I spent a year acting in Los Angeles, and God hit me like a freight train. Very clearly, He said to me, "You're a leader Brittany. You're either leading my people to heaven or hell." So, I quit my job as a casting assistant to do full-time ministry and church planting. I wanted to learn how to live life right, and the more I read my Bible and surrendered every part of my life to Jesus, the more my identity began to change. I knew that my life would have to change as well.

A year later, God brought me back to Isla Vista, and I was baptized. Drenched in my white dress, I was so proud to make the public declaration that Jesus is the lover of my soul. It was super undignified . . . and completely awesome. He's always been the lover of my soul, but today I'm letting Him be everything He promised He would be. When I realized, I mean fully realized, what it meant that Jesus died on the cross for my sins, I had to die with Him. So I got in that water and buried the successful, black, educated, well-read, attractive, self-hating, prideful, bitter, abused, lonely, sometimes kind of funny Muslim, Baptist, Seventh Day Adventist. As Jesus arose, I rose out of the water with Him, and He called me into a new life and a new identity as a daughter. Here I stand today, just a daughter, and more loved than ever before.

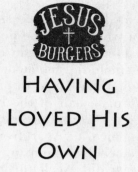

HAVING LOVED HIS OWN

BY NICOLE PAK

I hated my father. It was sort of a family tradition. My gentle and humble father had hated his father (my grandfather), who hated his father (my great-grandfather), who hated his father (my great great-grandfather). As far as I knew, when my relatives on my dad's side were hurting, we were not the sort to make a scene, preferring instead to express our hatred in well-mannered, socially acceptable ways, like coldly tolerating the parent's existence when necessary, and ignoring it the rest of the time. This hatred was consuming and powerful. Not the raging, pain-filled sort of hate that signifies sorrow over a lost love, but the cold ambivalence and quiet disdain of a heart so detached that it couldn't be less interested if the father lives or dies.

I had never been able to pinpoint a specific reason for hating my lovely father, and in fact, everyone else seemed to revere him. He was a kind, intelligent, and hardworking man, widely respected in our community and adored by my mother, but his very presence made me highly uncomfortable. When he talked to me, I wished he wouldn't. I was a bit relieved when, in my late teens, I learned my hatred was inherited— but what was to be done? I was beginning to notice that my hatred for my father was the source of several ills, including a blanket distrust of all men, an anxious hunch that I had to protect myself at all times from the male half of the human population who might at any second hurt me, and a bitterness that was rotting my soul. Apart from faithfully loving his wife and financially supporting his family, both of which my father did excellently, I didn't have the faintest idea what a father was supposed to do. Mine was nice, responsible, and distant, reading *Time* magazines during dinner and smiling pleasantly when my brother and I spoke to him—which wasn't often.

Partly because of the absence of a real relationship with a father, and partly because I had watched one too many Disney princess movies during my childhood, I came into college with some very interesting theology: instead of relationship, I had a business transaction—I give you what you want in exchange for what I want.

With God, I supposed He wanted good religious duties and high morals as proof of my devotion to Him. I could do that. I would live virtuously, and then God, like a fairy godmother or a magic genie, would reward my virtuous behavior with a picture-perfect happily ever after, complete with a lovely Christian husband whom I would meet in college. (I took some creative license when adjusting the Disney dream to my life). For someone who never verbally or explicitly confirmed this deal with God, I was remarkably attached to it, so much so that when I turned twenty, I had spent all of my life saying no to drinking, drugs, sex, and parties—at which any of the former were available—and instead had poured my efforts into being a studious, morally upright Christian; yet I still

I did not have the only dream I had ever dreamt of. I was devastated and confused beyond reason.

I had been waiting for twenty years for my payout, only to discover the entire bargain—and by association, the Party who had "offered" the bargain—was a sham. (For some inexplicable reason, it never occurred to me that God had never promised or agreed to my bargain, and that I was, indeed, the author of this brilliant commercial transaction.)

I had no concept of a God as a Father who would listen patiently to all of my disappointments and fears and walk me through my confusion with His love and truth. My relationship with my earthly father consisted of barely tolerating him. For all of his good manners, he was an intellectual and had little patience for irrational emotions. I knew there was no space for mistakes or pain with him, and I assumed the same was true with my Heavenly Father.

I didn't know where to turn. A life without God, the Source of all life, was utterly meaningless. But a life with a con artist of a God? That didn't interest me either. So I turned to other comforts that delivered on their promises. To numb the pain of disappointment, fear, rage, and confusion, I drugged myself with a newfound obsession with Fashion (a god who promised and delivered compliments from strangers), a Binging Disorder (a god who distracted me from my emotional pain with the physical pain that resulted from gorging myself with food until I felt sick), and wasted hours upon hours on the Internet (a god who kept my thoughts miles away from addressing the avalanche of issues in my life). I wasn't particularly fond of any of my new gods, but at least they met their end of our agreement—or so I thought. I wasn't expecting their close friends, Debilitating Depression, Self-Hatred, and Paranoia, but they made their home in me as well. I stopped sleeping, showering, and attending classes, and spent nearly every waking hour in bed, eating to self-harm while I stared at Facebook or watched sixteen straight hours of television online. I felt (and probably looked) like a zombie—a dead man walking. A few months passed in this vegetable state before I concluded my sophomore year at my university and realized I needed help.

I took three years off to heal at a ministry school and a discipleship training school, where God began to teach me how to be in relationship with Him instead of perpetually and unilaterally striking ridiculous bargains that had little to do with love and everything to do with fear and manipulation. He blessed me with the beginnings of a real relationship with Him, God the Father, and my earthly father, both of whom I started to trust, feel loved by, and love in return for the first time in my life.

During this season, I discovered there are implications to God calling Himself a Father. It means that He stands with me every moment, listens compassionately when I feel bitter and disappointed, carries my every small dream in His heart, shares His much larger dreams with me, disciplines me, loves me into freedom, delivers me from all of my fears, believes for and in me when everyone else, including me, has given up hope, empowers me with His Spirit, and shapes me into His Son's likeness—and that's not even the half of it!

I started to believe that God was not always and only disappointed in me, but that He, like most fathers, genuinely enjoys His child's presence, and that when He says He rejoices over me with gladness and singing, and quiets me by His love (Zephaniah 3:17), He is neither exaggerating nor manipulating. I saw that while my brokenness seemed impressive to me, it was not that impressive to God, and it was not so strong that it could withstand the mighty love of God. This love was powerful enough to deliver me from every lie that kept me in bondage, as my chains crumbled in its wake. I learned that God cares very much that I make wise choices, not so that I can manipulate Him into giving me what I think I want, but so that I might walk freely in relationship with Him, receiving of His truth, power, and love everyday.

It was during my first year of this three-year period that I made a visit to the Jesus Burgers house with my ministry school. During our several days with the Jesus Burgers house, I watched in wonder as young men and women my age tangibly and extravagantly demonstrated the love of God to strangers and friends (in varying states of sobriety) alike. The respect, care, and joy with which they approached strangers, asked questions about our lives, listened to our stories late into the night, prayed with us, prophesied over us, and opened their hearts and homes to us confounded me. I had often heard we should live the Gospel in addition to preaching it, but I had never before seen a ministry actually demonstrate the Gospel to their neighbors in a tangible and consistent way.

Over the next two years, God continued to reveal to me my identity in Him, and He replaced the lies that I believed about God, myself, and others with His truth. I knew God the Father and His Son Jesus had proved His love to humanity by willingly taking upon Himself all of our spiritual, physical, mental, and emotional torment, and by delivering us from every lie and fear with His death and resurrection. Building His Kingdom seemed like a much better way to live my life.

I had learned during my three-year break that the Great Commission Jesus gives in Matthew 28:16–20 to "go and make disciples of all nations" was actually the most fulfilling way to live. What is more wonderful than regularly feeling the unrelenting love of God for people who are made in His image?

I knew I wanted to spend the rest of my life experiencing the love of God in community, and introducing people to the Father whose love had already compelled Him to step into the most horrific depths of human depravity and draw us out of it once at the Cross. I had also heard that only 4 percent of all American university students were Christian, so I wanted to be a force of change with this almost unreached people group. I wanted young people, especially, to know that they were created to be free! I remembered a community that was doing this already—the Jesus Burgers ministry—and I wanted to be a part of it. This time, I transferred to the University of California, Santa Barbara, knowing that Jesus was alive and looking for people to receive His love, and that I could love them with Him.

I immersed myself in the community of Isla Vista and was intentional about being involved with Jesus Burgers. On one particular night, I was navigating my way through the Jesus Burgers house and saw a young man named Suraj from one of my classes. He was one of my favorite classmates. I felt affectionately like an older sister towards him since he was closer in age to my younger brother than to me. His personality reminded me of one of my favorite people in the world—my mother. He, like my mother, was genuine and warm. He was opinionated and quick to speak, but also humble, utterly unpretentious, and just as quick to acknowledge when he was wrong.

"Suraj!" I cried, weaving my way through the people to give him a hug.

"Nicole!" he slightly slurred, returning the hug.

I could smell the alcohol on his breath. I was so happy he was here! "What are you doing here?" I asked with a grin.

"Well, I thought there was a party here, but," he paused as he tried to focus his gaze, "I think I came to the wrong house. And," he pointed unstably towards the door, "all my friends just left."

"Haha, yeah, well there is a party of sorts here, but probably not the one you were looking for."

We sat down on the couch.

"What are you doing here?" Suraj asked.

"This is my church—we give out free burgers on Friday nights."

"Oh, cool. So you're a Christian?" Suraj inquired.

"Mhm. Do you have a religious background?" I asked.

"My family's Hindu," Suraj said, and then pointed to himself, "but I'm not really anything. I'm agnostic, I guess."

I felt the Father's joy over this young man, a fun-loving, genuine soul whom He had formed, whom He was intimately acquainted with, and whom He had created to know Him. After a few more minutes of conversation in which we talked about the likely existence of God or a higher power (which he insisted every person, even atheists, secretly believed, since there is no way to deny His or its existence), I asked if I could pray for him. When he answered in the affirmative, I had the privilege of blessing and speaking truth from the Father's heart. I blessed the man God created him to be, as well as every part of his life—his body, soul, mind, and spirit; his relationships, his family, and everything he put his hands to. I blessed him on his journey to discover the God who sees, knows, and loves him.

Afterwards, he thanked me and explained as he

pointed to his heart, "What you just did . . . it made me feel something, really deep and really good." I grinned again. That was the Father's love, and He is after His children!

Jesus is not blinded or shocked by the "bad behavior" of any of the students, but He sees and has compassion on the broken heart beneath that produces the symptoms. Just as the Father saw my depression, binging disorder, and shopping and Internet addictions as the symptoms of a broken and hurting person who was looking for a place to belong, for identity and worth, and a way to cope with the pain of a destructive lifestyle, I knew God saw the hearts of each of these sons and daughters He had created in His image to be loved by Him. Even when I thought I was beyond repair, God saw me, loved me, and honored me. I knew the Spirit of God was pursuing each young man and woman beside me.

Every time I biked or walked through the streets on a Friday night to the Jesus Burgers house, I felt a rush of joy flood my heart. I couldn't stop grinning at the lively young people brimming with energy, potential, and a heart longing to experience something that made them feel alive. They were looking for something, and Someone was looking for them! It was going to be a good night. And it always was.

HOME TO
HIM

MIKAELA MCLAUGHLIN

I came to Isla Vista in a way that is very different than most. Most nineteen-year-olds come to Isla Vista in search of something. For some it's a college degree, for others it's the perfect surf, for most it's one of the biggest party schools in the country. I came to Isla Vista on the run.

After flunking my freshman year of college at a small liberal arts school near Pittsburgh, I bought myself a one way ticket to Santa Barbara, California, instead of boarding a plane home to Miami for drug treatment. I didn't know anyone in Santa Barbara, or IV for that matter, I just knew from attending a water polo camp at USCB a few years prior that Santa Barbara was beautiful. Little did I know that flight was the beginning of God's relentless pursuit to bring me home to Him.

I didn't grow up in the church or in a religious family. On the contrary, I grew up in a house where we were told that religious people are weak and cowardly. My dad told us that people use religion as a crutch and that the only way to be successful and to get somewhere in life was to work hard and do it all yourself. It is no wonder why my earliest memories are of feeling alone and empty. When I was in middle school I attended youth group with a friend of mine from school. I gained a lot of knowledge about Jesus and His word. However, it took ten years for the message to travel the few short inches from my head to my heart where it really belonged. In those ten years, I was prey to misery, depression, an eating disorder, serious drug addiction, alcoholism, and guilt and shame from childhood sexual abuse.

I lived in IV for six months, and for four of them I was homeless. I was selling my body for drugs and hardly drew a sober breath. While roaming the streets of IV one day, I walked by a chain-link fence and was greeted by a happy golden retriever. His owners followed him to the fence. Shockingly, in this crazy college town I found his owners were a family. An actual family! Young kids! In Isla Vista! I petted the cute dog, said hello to the children, and wondered what the heck they were doing living in Isla Vista. Moments later, their father, Jason Lomelino, the pastor of IV Church and Jesus Burgers, came around the side of the house and told me that God loved me.

I was sure that this God that he spoke of had intended the message for someone else. I was sure that God didn't love the homeless junkie standing in front of him. I didn't respond, simply because I didn't know what to say, and I walked away. A few days later I met a girl who told me about Jesus Burgers, and she told me I should go get a burger there. She said there was food and love. Food and love were two things I hadn't had in a while, and somehow against everything in me, I went.

That night, I found myself walking up to to 6686 Del Playa Drive. I could smell burgers cooking, and felt a strange feeling in my stomach and my heart. As soon as I got in line for a burger, I got a feeling that I should run. At that moment, I audibly heard what I know now as the voice of God say, "Stay." I finally grabbed a burger, and it was handed to me by a guy my age with a huge smile on his face. Moments later, I fell to my knees, crying with the burger in my hand. Two girls came over to me and kindly asked me if they could pray for me. Broken and carrying such a heavy burden, I knew in that moment there was nothing left to do but oblige. These two girls rested their hands on my shoulders and whispered prayers in my ears. I can't remember the words they spoke, but I remember the feeling in my soul while they spoke them. For the first time in over a year, I was instantly sobered. I felt, finally, like I could rest. All of a sudden, I felt like I was going to be okay.

I got up and sat inside for about an hour with a few people who lived at the Jesus Burgers house. They shared the Gospel with me. They told me the Good News. They told me the Truth. And after they did, I told them my truth. My truth was that I believed God wanted nothing to do with me. I told them that after I got sober and cleaned up my act, I would give a relationship with God a chance. They told me that I didn't need to. They told me that God wanted to meet me right where I was that night. I had never heard that before.

What I encountered at Jesus Burgers was love. I didn't encounter religion or rules, just love. As the girl had promised, my stomach and my soul left there full. The new friends I had made invited me to Isla Vista Church for more food and more love. That Sunday as I approached the same chain link fence I had been at just a few days ago, it all made sense. That wasn't just a house, it was a church. And it wasn't just one family that lived there, the family of God dwelled there too. I walked inside the fence and just cried. I felt at home.

I attended church at IVC for about a month before I left to go back to the East Coast to try to get sober. Isla Vista Church helped carry the message I learned as a twelve-year-old girl from my head to my heart. The church family saw me as a precious daughter of the King, when all I could see was a pathetic, lonely junkie. God used my time in IV to reach me in a way that I don't believe would have been possible if I hadn't encountered the love I felt at Jesus Burgers and IVC. That time redefined what religion and Christianity meant to me. Spending time with the IVC family and at Jesus Burgers made me want what they had. The encounters I had there melted the icy dark shadows in which I had lived and shivered for so long.

When I finally got sober, I got plugged into a church where I now live in South Florida, and I gave my life to my true Father. One night in May 2014 in a moment of prayer, God showed me a clear picture of me and my husband, Brian, serving together in Isla Vista. Two days after God showed me this image, Jason posted a Facebook status about an internship program at Isla Vista Church. After talking to Jason, Brian and I knew that God was calling us to go learn and serve with the IVC family and to live in community with them for about two months. God called me back to the church and the people who taught me about God's relentless love and amazing grace. He did this so that Brian and I can grow as believers and develop a plan to build a ministry in South Florida that will reach people the way Jesus Burgers reached me.

I believe that God has intentionally used and will continue to use each one of my hurts for His glory and to bring home more of His children who can't